OECD ECONOMIC SURVEYS

UNITED STATES

DOCUMENTS OFFICIELS

1979

GOVERNMENT
PUBLICATIONS

ORGANISATION FOR ECONOMIC CO-OPERATION AND DEVELOPMENT

The Organisation for Economic Co-operation and Development (OECD) was set up under a Convention signed in Paris on 14th December, 1960, which provides that the OECD shall promote policies designed:

— *to achieve the highest sustainable economic growth and employment and a rising standard of living in Member countries, while maintaining financial stability, and thus to contribute to the development of the world economy;*

— *to contribute to sound economic expansion in Member as well as non-member countries in the process of economic development;*

— *to contribute to the expansion of world trade on a multilateral, non-discriminatory basis in accordance with international obligations.*

The Members of OECD are Australia, Austria, Belgium, Canada, Denmark, Finland, France, the Federal Republic of Germany, Greece, Iceland, Ireland, Italy, Japan, Luxembourg, the Netherlands, New Zealand, Norway, Portugal, Spain, Sweden, Switzerland, Turkey, the United Kingdom and the United States.

The Socialist Federal Republic of Yugoslavia is associated in certain work of the OECD, particularly that of the Economic and Development Review Committee.

*
**

The annual review of the United States
by the OECD Economic and Development Review Committee
took place on 18th June 1975.

The present Survey has been updated subsequently.

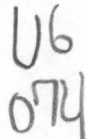

CONTENTS

DIAGRAMS

INTRODUCTION

The last two years have seen a marked slowdown or decline in activity going hand-in-hand with the worst inflation experienced since the early 1950's. Following the restoration of better price stability in 1972, due in part to the temporary effects of price-wage controls, strong domestic demand pressures and worldwide shortages of food and other primary commodities during the 1972/73 boom gave rise to a marked acceleration of inflation that was seriously aggravated by the steep rise in oil prices. However, the strongest declines in activity and resource utilisation since the Second World War brought the rise in prices down towards a more acceptable level.

In view of the progress made in reducing inflation and the sharp rise in unemployment, demand management has been changed towards stimulating activity. Given the large tax cuts and the easing of monetary policy it would seem reasonable to expect an upturn in activity in the second half of the year and recent indicators support this expectation. During the next year and beyond, speed and flexibility of policy reaction may be needed to combine a recovery of activity sufficient to reduce unemployment with further progress towards better price stability.

The present Survey focuses attention on the factors behind the high inflation and the closely coincident severe recession (Part I), and on propects for recovery of activity over the next twelve months (Part II). Issues related to fiscal stimulus, large budget deficits and their implications for debt management and monetary policy are considered in Part III, and Part IV summarizes the main conclusions of the Survey.

I RECESSION AND INFLATION

Review of Major Developments

The international boom which began in 1972 reached its peak in the US in the first half of 1973. While inflation partly delayed by price controls was still accelerating, real domestic demand, particularly housing investment and consumer durables purchases, already showed signs of weakening before the outbreak of the oil crisis. Final demand fell markedly in the fourth quarter of 1973 and the first quarter of 1974, with especially large declines in the sales of autos and energy related products. In the second and third quarters economic activity appeared to steady somewhat but did not regain the levels of 1973. Inflation, however, continued virtually unabated as fuel prices jumped and the termination of controls in April allowed expression of already existing price pressures. While views were divided as to the momentum of a new upswing, there was wide agreement among forecasters within and outside the Administration that a recovery was likely to take place in the second half of the year.

The period of relative demand stability was followed by an abrupt weakening of activity in the last quarter of 1974. Real consumption, heavily influenced by the near collapse of auto sales, fell sharply and was the main factor in a massive involuntary increase in inventories. Private non-residential investment, hitherto an element of strength, contracted drastically and residential investment continued its downward spiral.   The slide of output and employment picked up speed in the first quarter of 1975 as the process of inventory liquidation got under way.   With the pass-through of earlier price increases and the sharp decline in demand, inflation began to slow significantly in the winter of 1974-75, remaining, however, substantially above the levels of the previous decade.   At the time of writing the recession appears to be bottoming out, and there are tentative indications of a near-term recovery.

A number of features distinguish the current recession from others of the post-war period.   There is disagreement as to the timing of the cyclical downswing, as the situation was complicated by the oil crisis, and some demand ele-

Diagram 1   Output and Employment

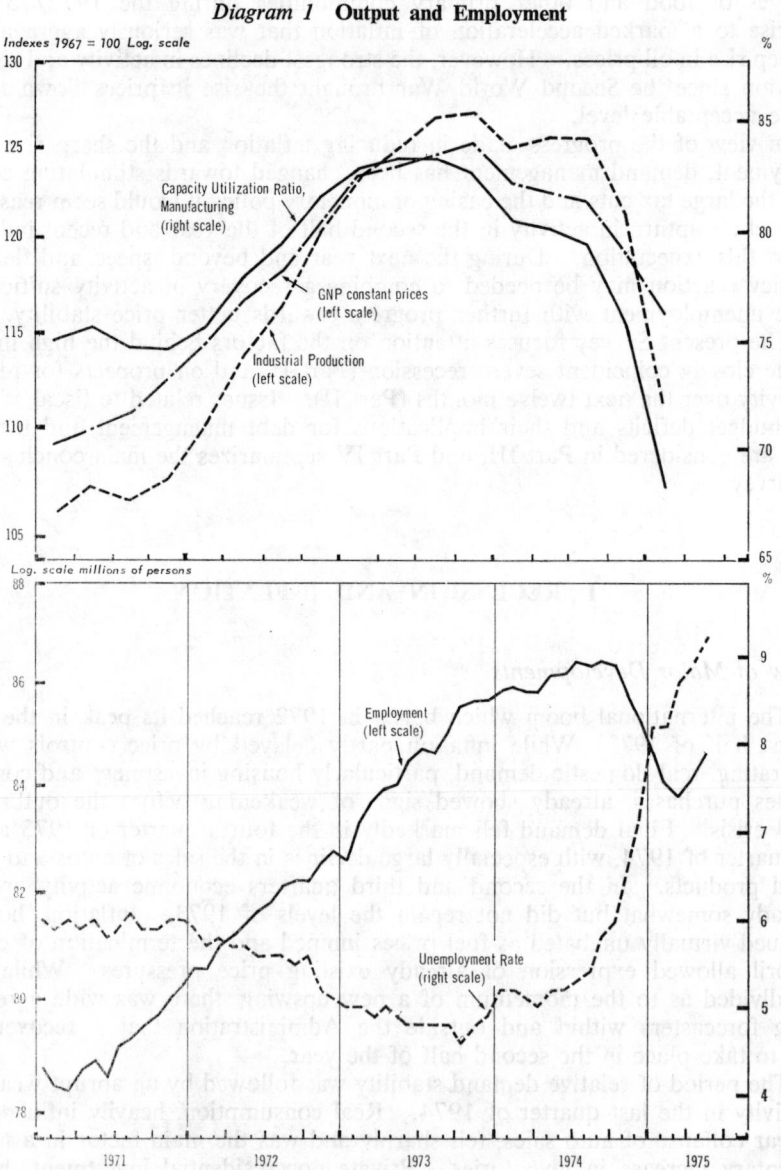

Source: Dept. of Commerce, *Business Conditions Digest.*

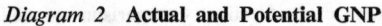

Diagram 2 **Actual and Potential GNP**

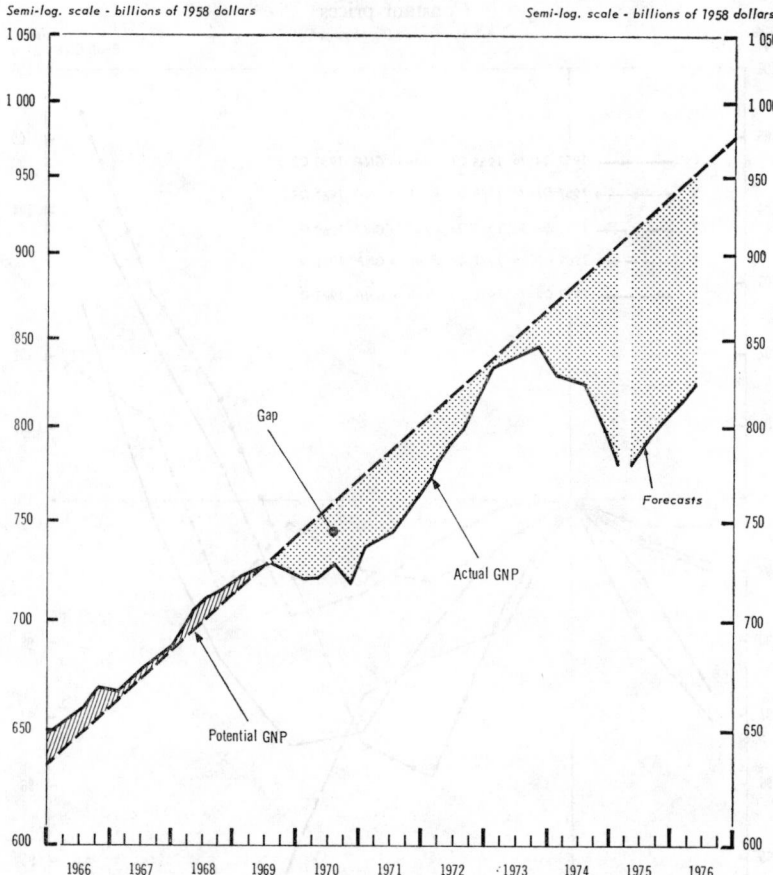

Source: Dept. of Commerce, *Business Conditions Digest* and OECD Secretariat.

ments, particularly investment, remained strong until well into the third quarter of 1974. But whatever its dating, it is by far the most severe of the post-war recessions. Through May 1975 the decline in industrial production from the 1973 peak amounted to 14.4 per cent and capacity utilization in manufacturing dropped to 68.5 per cent in the first quarter, both post-war records. Unemployment reached 9.2 per cent of the labour force in May, again a record (Diagrams 1 and 2). The decline in real GNP has been both more prolonged and more profound than in previous recessions (Diagram 3). In addition to its duration and depth the current recessionary period has had a number of other exceptional features.

First, a historically high rate of inflation co-existed with the severe recession. In spite of some moderation of inflation beginning in late 1974, the increase in the GNP deflator and in the consumer price index in 1974 taken as a whole was the highest in the post-war period. Inflation had already reached rather high rates in the fourth quarter of 1973 in spite of the price controls (Diagram 4). With the increase in fuel prices and the termination of the controls in April, measured inflation accelerated to double digit figures and did not begin to subside to more manageable levels until 1975. Although the overall rate of inflation

Diagram 3   Cyclical Comparisons of GNP
Constant prices

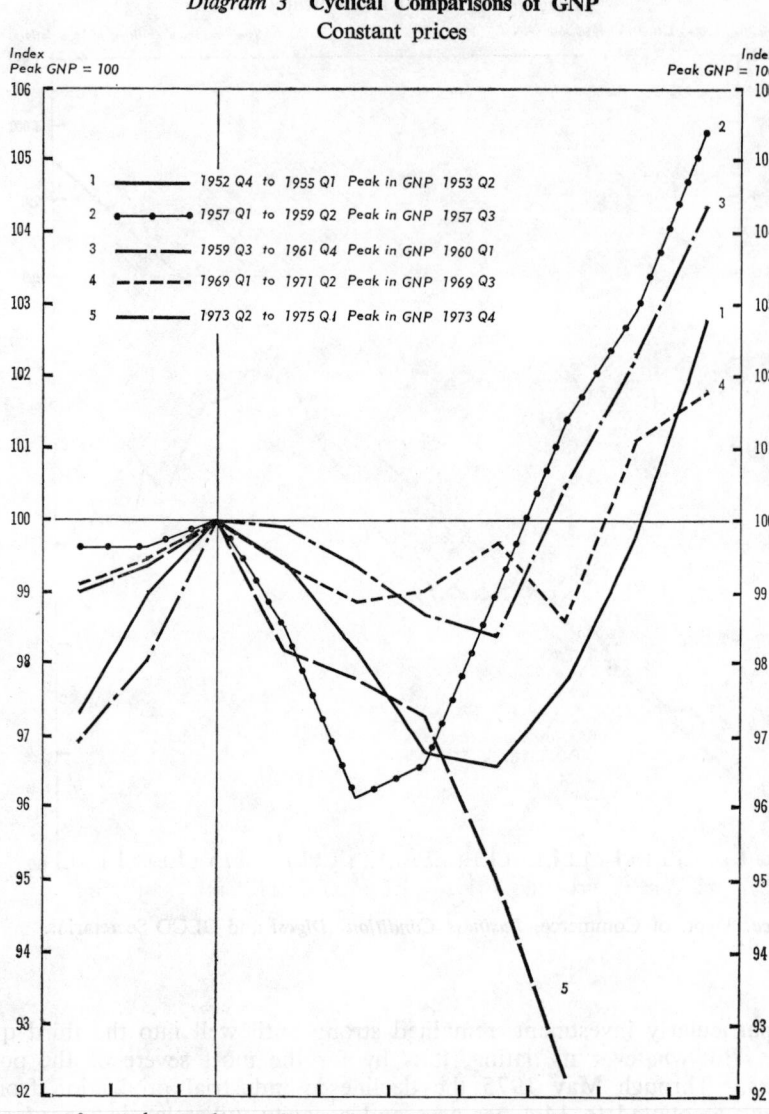

changed little during the year, the movement of price components varied considerably. At the wholesale level, farm product prices showed an erratic behaviour, while industrial commodity prices maintained a more steady advance. Within the latter group, crude materials led the price increases in the first two quarters and these increases showed up in intermediate goods prices in the second and third quarters. In the last quarter of 1974 and the first five months of 1975, final product prices continued to rise, though at a slowing pace, while crude and intermediate materials prices recorded declines or marked decelerations. The commodity component of consumer prices followed a similar pattern, but the service components showed an even greater resistance to rapidly weakening demand than typically observed during earlier recessions.

Table 1 Demand and Output

Percentage changes, seasonally adjusted annual rates, of demand components in constant 1958 prices

| | Annual | | | Quarterly | | | | | | | | 1975 |
	1972	1973	1974	1973 Q1	Q2	Q3	Q4	1974 Q1	Q2	Q3	Q4	Q1
Personal consumption	6.2	4.7	-2.3	8.1	.6	1.2	-6.4	-4.7	2.2	3.4	-13.2	2.5
Durables	13.4	8.3	-9.2	28.4	-5.0	-4.8	-22.6	-7.3	6.2	3.8	-45.1	10.8
Non-durables and services	4.6	3.8	-.5	3.6	2.0	3.0	-1.9	-4.1	1.2	3.4	-3.6	.6
Private fixed investment	11.5	7.9	-7.3	17.8	4.2	-2.2	-5.8	-9.5	-1.6	-13.9	-24.8	-27.9
Non-residential	9.1	12.8	-.4	25.0	9.4	3.4	3.8	1.3	.8	-9.6	-19.3	-22.1
Residential	17.9	-4.1	-27.1	2.3	-9.9	-16.5	-30.2	-38.4	-10.2	-28.9	-44.2	-48.3
Government purchases of goods and services	2.7	.8	1.1	3.1	-.6	-.6	5.7	.8	-.5	.3	1.1	3.9
Federal	.2	-6.1	-1.4	-2.0	-7.9	-10.0	1.4	-.7	.0	1.4	3.6	2.8
State and local	4.7	6.0	2.9	6.9	4.8	6.2	8.5	1.8	-.9	-.4	-.4	4.1
Final domestic demand	6.3	4.5	-2.5	8.6	.9	.4	-4.3	-4.5	1.1	.0	-12.5	-2.0
Inventory investment[1]	.2	.5	-.3	-.7	.2	.1	5.7	-4.4	-1.2	-1.5	2.9	-11.2
Total domestic demand	6.5	4.9	-2.7	7.8	1.2	.5	1.4	-8.7	-.0	-1.5	-9.8	-12.7
Net exports[1]	-.3	1.0	.5	1.6	1.0	1.1	1.0	1.7	-1.5	-.5	.8	1.3
Exports	7.0	19.6	8.0	45.5	7.0	6.2	12.5	28.1	.5	-12.9	-5.5	-15.6
Imports	11.5	5.6	1.5	17.5	-6.2	-8.1	-.7	5.4	23.1	-8.9	-15.9	-32.5
GNP	6.1	5.9	-2.1	9.5	2.2	1.6	2.3	-7.0	-1.6	-1.9	-9.0	-11.3
GNP Deflator	3.4	5.6	10.3	5.5	7.3	8.3	8.6	12.3	9.4	11.9	14.4	8.5

1 Change in inventory investment/net exports as per cent of GNP of previous period, annual rate.

Source: Department of Commerce, Survey of Current Business.

Secondly, real private consumption fell very sharply and was a leading element in the downswing of the economy. In previous business downturns consumption constituted an element of stability, declining only slightly or even continuing to increase (Table 2). The sharp decline of consumption between 1973 and 1974 conceals, however, the rather erratic movements during this period (Diagram 5).

The steep fall in the winter 1973-74 was followed by slight increases in the second and third quarters and the renewed drop in the fourth quarter gave way to some recovery in the early months of 1975. While this volatile pattern is to a large degree attributable to developments in auto sales, real spending on items except for services was also rather erratic. A third factor has been the decline in residential construction, unprecedented in terms of its depth and (for reasons explained later) rather resistant to easing monetary conditions. Indeed,

Diagram 4a **Price Movements**
Percentage increases at annual rates

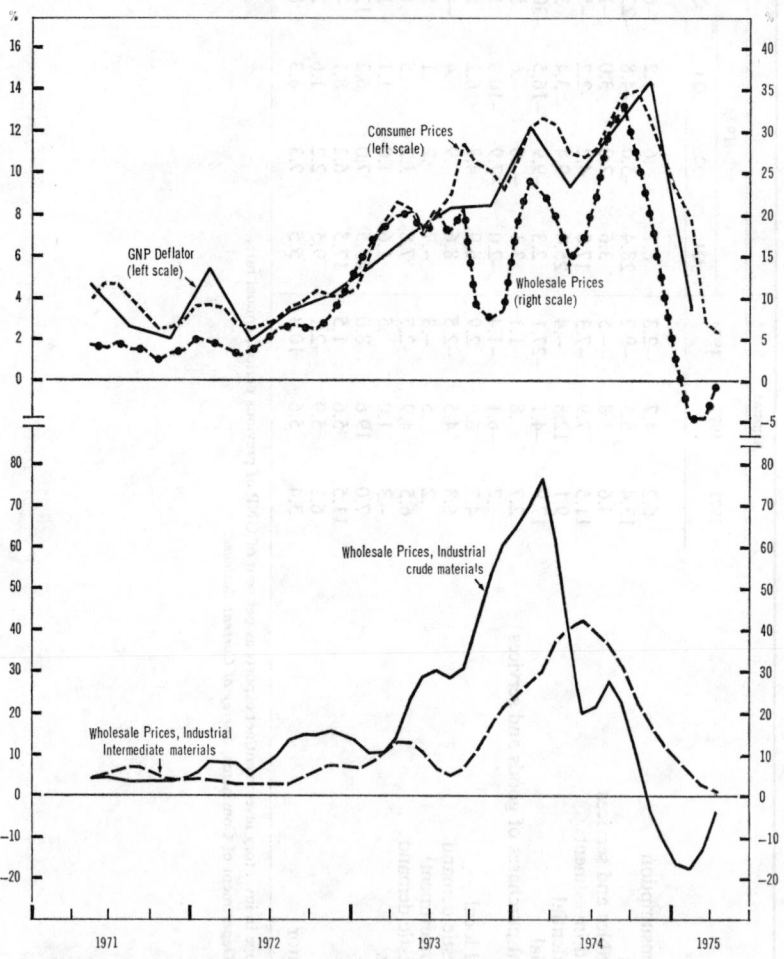

NOTE Wholesale and consumer price changes are percentage increases of 3-month moving averages over 3-months earlier at annual rates. All data are seasonally adjusted except the service component of consumer prices, which has no clear seasonal pattern.

Source: Dept. of Commerce, *Survey of Current Business.*

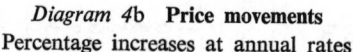

Diagram 4b **Price movements**
Percentage increases at annual rates

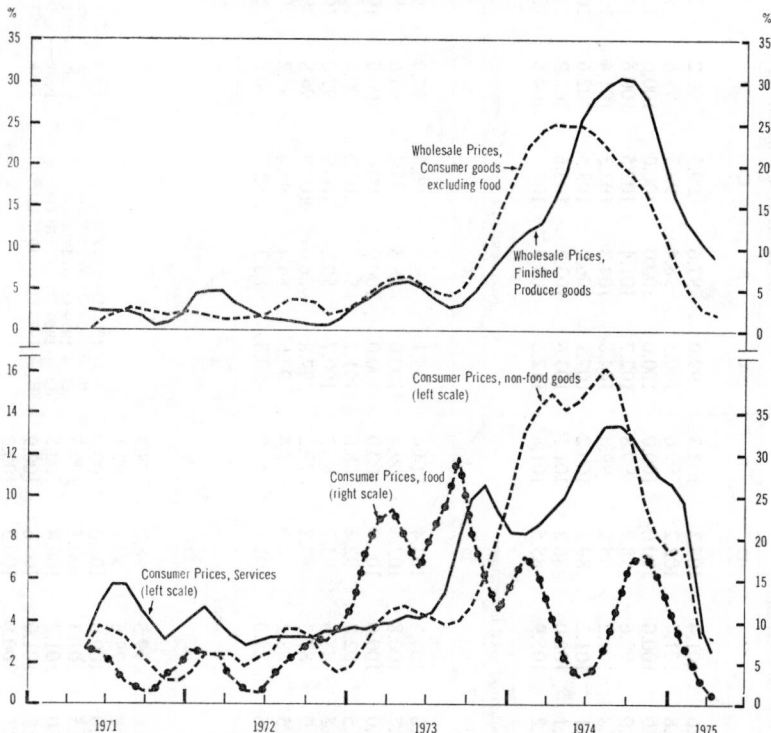

NOTE Wholesale and consumer price movements are percentage increase of 3-month moving averages over 3-months earlier at annual rates. All data are seasonally adjusted except service component of consumer prices, which has no clear seasonal pattern.

Source: Dept. of Commerce, *Survey of Current Business.*

residential investment, falling in real terms to the lowest absolute level since the immediate post-war period, has been even weaker than real household expenditure[1]. After hitting a peak in the spring of 1973 private housing starts began a sharp fall only briefly interrupted in early 1974 (Diagram 6). In contrast to the sharp rebounds of earlier recessions, housing investment remained unresponsive to the improvement in mortgage conditions after the summer of 1974, though very recently housing starts and permits have turned up.

Another specific feature of the current recession was the fact that the weakening in consumer demand and housing did not spread to non-residential fixed investment and inventory accumulation until well after the peak in real GNP in 1973. This factor, a reason for caution in describing 1974 in its entirety as a recession period, meant that the drastic cuts in production and employment appeared only long after the weakening of final demand. Business investment continued to increase in real terms through the first half of 1974. Investment intentions generally remained buoyant and new orders for durable goods continued to rise markedly through the summer (Diagram 6). Probably more important to the maintenance of employment and output, business continued to build up large

1 Housing starts fell to annual rates of than one million units, whereas the formation of households in the US is around 1.5 million per year. In addition, the average annual demolition or renovation rate can be put at approximately ¾ to ¼ million units.

Table 2   Demand, Output and Employment During Post-War Recessions

Pre-recession GNP peak quarter (0 quarter) = 100 (in 1958 prices)

GNP

	A	B	C	D	E
−2	97.3	99.6	96.9	99.1	99.0
−1	99.0	99.6	98.0	99.5	99.4
0	100.0	100.0	100.0	100.0	100.0
+1	99.4	98.5	99.9	99.4	98.2
+2	98.2	96.1	99.4	98.9	97.8
+3	96.8	96.6	98.7	99.0	97.3
+4	96.6	99.0	98.4	99.7	95.1
+5	97.8	101.4	100.5	98.6	92.3

Private consumption

	A	B	C	D	E
−2	98.1	99.1	98.8	99.1	101.4
−1	99.4	99.2	98.8	100.0	101.7
0	100.0	100.0	100.0	100.0	100.0
+1	99.8	100.1	101.2	100.6	98.8
+2	99.6	98.7	100.8	101.0	99.3
+3	99.7	99.4	100.8	101.7	100.2
+4	100.7	100.9	100.8	102.4	96.7
+5	102.1	102.0	102.1	101.7	97.3

Industrial production

	A	B	C	D	E
−2	96.6	100.9	93.9	98.1	98.3
−1	98.7	99.7	94.3	98.9	99.7
0	100.0	100.0	100.0	100.0	100.0
+1	99.9	95.8	97.8	99.1	98.3
+2	95.2	90.4	96.2	96.8	98.8
+3	92.2	88.9	93.9	96.6	98.8
+4	91.9	93.5	92.5	96.0	95.5
+5	92.4	97.8	96.2	93.0	87.8

Federal expenditures

	A	B	C	D	E
−2	92.8	101.6	101.4	105.3	102.3
−1	96.4	101.8	101.4	102.2	99.6
0	100.0	100.0	100.0	100.0	100.0
+1	100.1	100.0	99.6	98.9	99.8
+2	88.5	101.8	101.2	95.2	99.8
+3	80.8	104.1	102.0	89.2	100.2
+4	77.2	105.1	105.9	86.3	101.1
+5		107.2		85.5	101.8

Residential fixed investment

	A	B	C	D	E
−2	98.0	104.0	104.2	103.4	114.4
−1	100.0	101.5	100.8	103.8	109.4
0	100.0	100.0	100.0	100.0	100.0
+1	97.0	100.5	92.8	92.4	88.6
+2	96.5	99.5	88.6	93.7	86.2
+3	99.0	99.0	87.3	87.8	79.2
+4	106.0	104.5	88.2	92.0	67.4
+5	112.6	114.6	89.0	101.7	57.0

Employment

	A	B	C	D	E
−2	98.9	99.8	99.5	98.7	98.3
−1	100.9	99.8	99.6	99.3	99.1
0	100.0	100.0	100.0	100.0	100.0
+1	99.7	99.5	101.3	100.5	100.3
+2	98.7	98.0	101.2	100.8	100.5
+3	98.3	97.7	101.0	100.6	100.9
+4	97.8	98.1	100.8	100.5	100.2
+5	97.7	98.9	100.6	100.5	98.3

State and local expenditures

	A	B	C	D	E
−2	99.0	97.6	99.3	98.2	96.5
−1	100.3	98.4	99.3	99.6	98.0
0	100.0	100.0	100.0	100.0	100.0
+1	102.7	101.4	102.5	100.6	100.4
+2	104.8	104.8	102.3	101.4	100.2
+3	107.9	106.0	103.5	102.6	100.1
+4	103.6	103.2	106.6	103.9	100.0
+5	112.0	109.7	106.3	104.5	101.0

Non-residential fixed investment

	A	B	C	D	E
−2	95.1	99.4	96.8	97.9	98.2
−1	100.0	98.5	96.4	98.0	99.1
0	100.0	100.0	100.0	100.0	100.0
+1	101.7	96.7	102.2	97.0	100.3
+2	100.7	90.2	100.9	96.8	100.5
+3	97.8	86.0	100.9	96.8	98.0
+4	97.8	84.4	96.4	97.2	92.9
+5	98.8	86.3	95.7	90.9	87.3

A = 1952 Q4 to 1954 Q3	Peak = 1953 Q2
B = 1957 Q1 to 1958 Q4	Peak = 1957 Q3
C = 1959 Q3 to 1961 Q2	Peak = 1960 Q1
D = 1969 Q1 to 1970 Q4	Peak = 1969 Q3
E = 1973 Q2 to 1975 Q1	Peak = 1973 Q4

Source: Department of Commerce, *Business Conditions Digest.*

Diagram 5 Indicators of Consumption

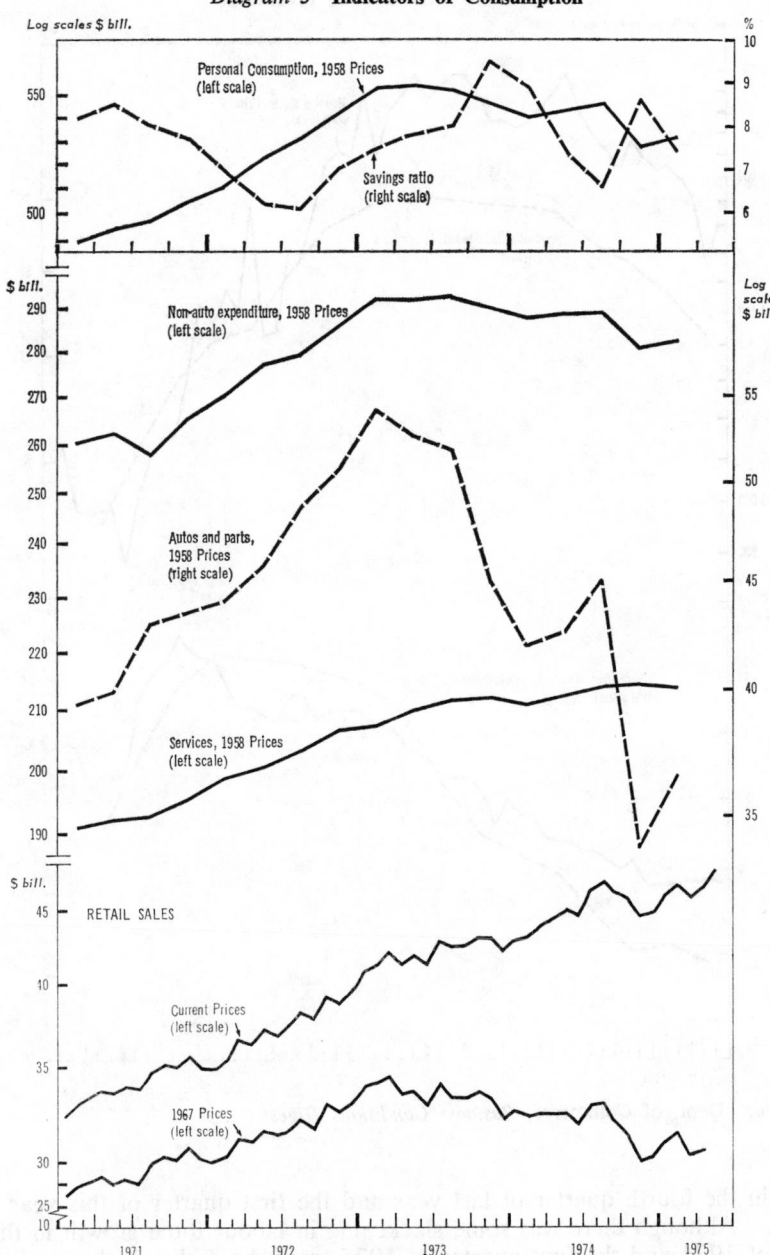

Source: Dept. of Commerce, *Survey of Current Business.*

inventories in spite of the palpable weakness of final demand. This resulted in a large rise in the inventory-sales ratio beginning in 1973 (Diagram 7). However, business investment intentions turned down sharply in the autumn, entailing a rapid decline of non-residential fixed investment. With the level of inventories increasingly out of proportion with sagging sales, production and employment dropped

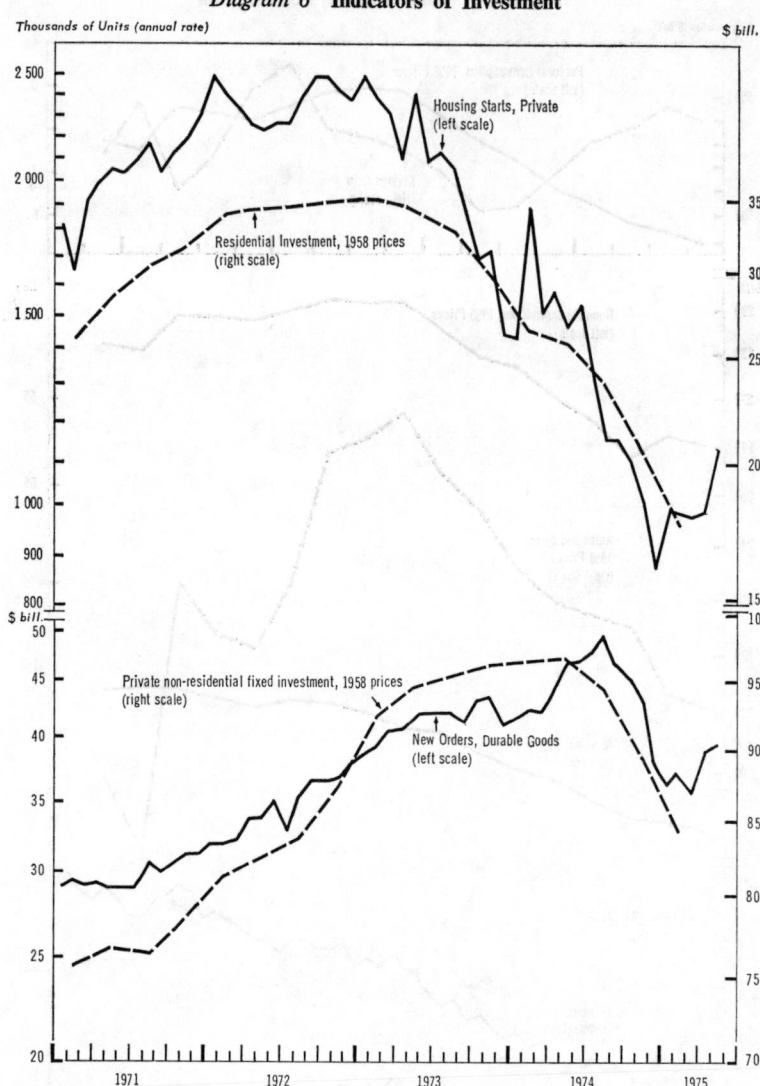

Diagram 6 **Indicators of Investment**

Source: Dept. of Commerce, *Business Conditions Digest.*

sharply in the fourth quarter of last year and the first quarter of this year (Diagram 1). Although there was some slackening in labour force growth in the last quarter of 1974 and the first quarter of 1975 from the earlier high rates, unemployment, especially among construction and manufacturing workers, reached very high levels (Table 3). Some recovery in total employment took place in April, but was not sufficient to prevent a further rise in the unemployment rate.

Causes of Persistent Inflation

The international boom which peaked in 1973, as well as the oil crisis and temporary food shortages, entailed spectacular, in some cases unprecedented, increases in commodity prices. The observed lags in price movements according

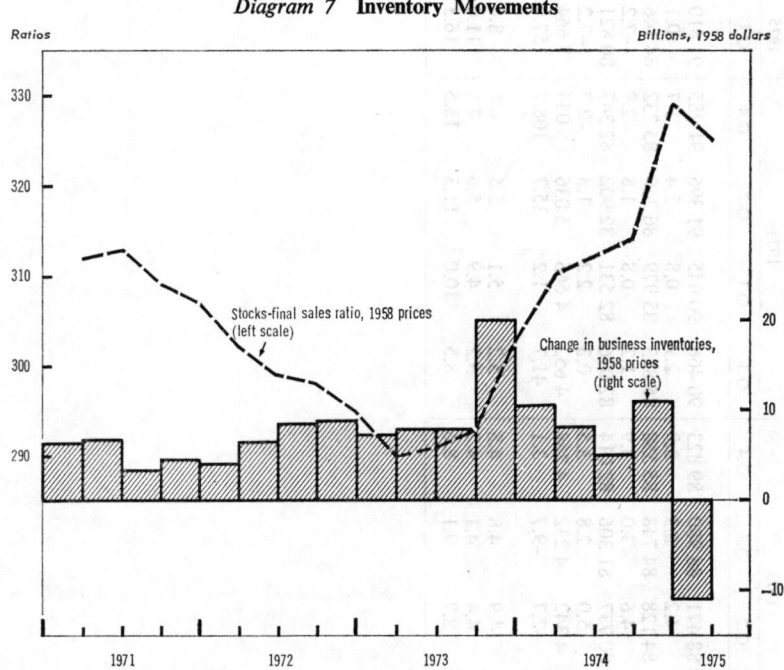

Diagram 7 **Inventory Movements**

Source: Dept. of Commerce, *Survey of Current Business.*

to stages of processing suggest that the gradual pass-through of these price increases was one of the major factors behind the high rate of inflation in 1974. The existence of price controls until April 1974 undoubtedly affected the timing of the pass-through and indeed tranferred much of the inflation problem from 1973 to 1974. The higher oil price, with its strong direct and indirect inflationary effects, was the single most important element in these higher input costs. Though domestic oil in principle remained subject to price controls, about one-third of domestic production (mainly new and stripper oil) was allowed to follow the international market price. Prices of other energy sources, influenced by oil prices, also increased sharply. The result was a 29.3 per cent rise in energy prices at the consumer level between 1973 and 1974. Allowing for indirect effects, the oil price rise alone probably added two percentage points to the consumer price index in 1974.

Although demand in the aggregate was weak after late 1973, excess demand in individual sectors seems to have contributed to the price acceleration in the first half of 1974. Capacity utilisation rates in major material industries, though declining, remained high by past standards during the first half of the year as orders piled up and structural shortages still prevailed. The resulting sharp increases in prices, especially after de-control, meant large profit increases in certain industries such as chemicals, paper and steel, though in some cases this represented only a restoration of profit margins existing prior to controls[2]. In view of the inflationary expectations and the fears of renewed price controls, it seems probable that some industries raised prices above the levels that could be explained by increased costs and/or demand pressures.

---

2 In contrast, in consumption-related industries such as textiles and appliances manufacturing, where demand was weak and capacity utilisation rates were low, price increases were more moderate.

Table 3 Labour Market

Thousands of persons

	1971	1972	1973	1974	1973				1974				1975
					Q.1	Q.2	Q.3	Q.4	Q.1	Q.1	Q.2	Q.4	Q.1
Civilian labour force[1]	84 113	86 542	88 714	91 011	87 570	88 471	88 980	89 823	90 466	90 645	91 396	91 785	91 810
Percentage increase[2]	1.7	2.9	2.5	2.6	2.1	4.2	2.3	3.9	2.9	0.8	3.4	1.7	0.1
Employed[1]	79 120	81 702	84 409	85 936	83 198	84 128	84 748	85 558	85 813	85 979	86 360	85 732	84 146
Percentage increase[2]	0.6	3.3	3.3	1.8	3.4	4.6	3.0	3.9	1.2	0.8	1.8	-2.9	-7.2
Non agricultural[1]	75 732	78 230	80 957	82 443	79 767	80 737	81 306	82 014	82 076	82 531	82 902	82 347	80 821
Percentage increase[2]	0.8	3.3	3.5	1.8	4.3	5.0	2.8	3.5	0.3	2.2	1.8	-2.7	-7.2
Unemployed[1]	4 993	4 840	4 304	5 076	4 372	4 342	4 232	4 264	4 652	4 666	5 036	6 053	7 664
Percentage increase[2]	22.1	-3.1	-11.1	17.9	-20.0	-2.7	-9.7	3.1	41.7	1.2	35.7	108.7	157.0
Percentage unemployment total[1]	5.9	5.6	4.9	5.6	5.0	4.9	4.8	4.8	5.2	5.1	5.5	6.6	8.4
Percentage unemployment manufacturing[1]	6.8	5.6	4.3	5.7	4.6	4.4	4.1	4.2	5.2	4.9	5.6	7.6	11.0
Percentage unemployment construction[1]	10.4	10.3	8.8	10.6	8.7	8.7	9.1	8.6	8.5	10.0	11.3	13.5	16.3

1 Seasonally adjusted.
2 Annual rate.
Source: Department of Commerce, Survey of Current Business.

Wage increases appear to have been a lagging rather than a leading element in inflation over the past period. Despite the acceleration in consumer prices, wage increases remained fairly modest until early 1974, advancing at rates of 6½-7 per cent (Diagram 8). An acceleration to well over 10 per cent occurred after the expiration of controls in April. Nevertheless, inflation advanced still more rapidly, resulting in further declines in real compensation and in the ratio of unit labour costs to product prices in manufacturing. The nominal wage increases

Diagram 8 **Wages, Productivity and Unit Labour Costs**
Percentage increases, annual rate

of 8.1 per cent for 1974 as a whole (measured by hourly earnings of workers in manufacturing) was the lowest of the major OECD countries, and the US was the sole country in which there was a decline in real earnings (Table 4). However, due to substantial decreases in output per man-hour, as well as accelerating wage rates, unit labour costs rose sharply in the course of the year. These cost increases probably sustained the advance in prices during the latter part of 1974. Deeply rooted inflationary expectations as well as certain fears of a new wage/price freeze have probably added to the difficulty of reducing inflation.

Table 4   **Price and Wage Behaviour in Major OECD Countries in 1974**

	Consumer Prices	Nominal Wages[1]	Real Wages	Unit Labour Costs
United States	11.0	8.1	–2.6	8.9
Canada	10.9	13.4	2.3	10.0
Japan	24.5	26.3	1.4	27.4
France	13.7	18.6	4.3	15.0
Germany	7.0	11.0	2.7	11.9
Italy	19.1	22.4	2.8	20-22
United Kingdom	16.0	17.0	0.9	18.5

1   Hourly earnings in manufacturing.
Source: OECD Secretariat.

Nevertheless, sagging demand finally did exert a dampening influence on inflation even though, considering the severeness of the recession, the response was both weak and belated. With economic slack increasing rapidly in the fourth quarter of 1974 and the first quarter of 1975 and with falling raw material prices, relatively rigid wholesale and consumer prices of finished industrial goods also began to decelerate. Most notable in the auto industry, price discounting spread even to highly administered price structures. Along with stabilising or falling food prices and some moderation of service prices, the advance of the consumer price index slowed to an annual rate of around 7 per cent in the first five months of 1975. Thus two years of efforts to stabilise prices showed some results, though at very high costs in lost production and employment.

Recession and its causes

A number of special features combined with the usual cyclical pattern of a business downswing to produce the most severe recession since the thirties :
(*i*)   the maintenance of a rather tight policy stance and its unexpectedly severe effects ;
(*ii*)   the commodity price boom and the strong resistance of inflation to weakening demand pressure ;
(*iii*)   the oil crisis and its repercussions on demand.

These factors are of course causally inter-related. The oil embargo and the associated price rise had a deflationary demand and output impact, and at the same time contributed to the general inflation, which in turn had recessionary effects through fiscal drag and real wage restraint. Inflation also served as a boost to interest rates and prompted the authorities to maintain a very restrictive policy stance until there were clear signs of deceleration. Consequently, the above factors cannot be considered as operating independently. Nevertheless, for purposes of the discussion they are first treated individually and then their combined influence on various demand components is considered.

(a) The energy crisis

The economic effects of the energy crisis can be separated into the temporary but strong impact of the oil embargo and the enduring impact of the oil price rise. The oil embargo resulted in a 20 per cent decline in the volume of oil imports in the first quarter of 1974. Although negative effects on production were largely avoided, perhaps partly due to the allocation programme of the Administration. severe shortages of gasoline and fuel occurred. Given furthermore the expectations of major fuel price increases, there was a steep decline in demand for automobiles and energy related goods and services. Indeed, the $10.6 billion fall in personal consumption (annual rate, 1958 prices) from the third quarter of 1973 to the first quarter of 1974 was more than accounted for by automobiles and energy. Business fixed capital formation was also affected, since a certain percentage of automobile sales, as well as truck sales, are attributed to business fixed investment. Thus during the initial phase, the oil crisis appears to have had a temporary, strong restraining influence on demand.

The role of the rise in fuel prices in the continuing downturn in the economy is less clear. The higher price for imported oil had an effect similar to an excise tax and resulted in a gross outflow of " purchasing power " of about $20 billion at an annual rate[3], equal to 1.3 per cent of GNP. Applying a multiplier of 1.5, GNP would have been reduced by perhaps two percentage points. While sizeable, this is much less than for most Member countries (Table 5). Furthermore, much of the impact was offset by increased exports of goods and services which may be considered as rather closely linked to the oil price increase [4]. As for the change in relative prices, in principle the result would be only to redirect spending from fuel and its complementary goods, particularly automobiles, to other goods and services. In practice, the adjustment might take some time and a temporary cutback of total demand would occur. This should have shown up as an increase in the household savings ratio, which available data, however, do not confirm (Diagram 5).

Table 5   **Impact of Oil Price Increase in Major OECD Countries**
Outflow of income resulting from oil price increase

	Outflow[1] in 1974 ($ bill.)	% of GNP
United States	19	1.3
Japan	15¼	3.5
France	7¼	2.7
Germany	8	2.1
Italy	7	4.7
United Kingdom	7	3.7

1 Under the assumption of no change in import volume from the previous year.
Source: OECD Secretariat.

(b) The deflationary demand effect of inflation

Inflation may exert a dampening effect on total demand in several ways. The most obvious result of inflation is that it erodes consumer income in real

---

3   Assuming no change in the volume of oil imports.
4   As discussed below, exports and imports of goods and services increased in 1974 by almost an identical amount ($ 41.7 billion vs. $ 42.8 billion). Of the increase in exports, about $ 6.5 billion was associated with petroleum transactions (a $ 3 billion increase in exports to OPEC countries, and a $ 3.5 billion increase net petroleum-related investment income).

terms but this does not necessarily imply that total demand is decreased, since the loss of one sector is a gain for another. There are, however, various ways in which inflation can dampen real demand. First, income may be shifted in favour of individuals or sectors with lower propensities to spend on domestic goods and services. Second, uncertainty as to future real income may discourage spending at the household level. A third important factor may be the wealth effect, as inflation diminishes the real value of financial assets. Finally, demand management policies are usually tightened in response to persistent or accelerating inflation even in the absence of excess demand conditions.

The redistributive effect of inflation is obvious when inflation is generated by a rise in import prices. The most prominent case — the oil price rise — has already been discussed. The rise in import prices of raw materials in 1973 may have had a deflationary impact as well, but this seems to have been offset by the rise in export prices of agricultural and other goods, since the non-oil terms of trade were practically unchanged. On the domestic side, there was an important redistribution of income from the general consuming public to the agricultural sector due to the sharp rise in food prices. Farm income increased from 1972 to 1973 by $17.5 billion, a magnitude comparable to the income outflow induced by the oil price increase. Partly attributable to the rise in export prices, the redistribution of income to the agricultural sector may have had a dampening effect on total demand through 1973 and early 1974, since the decline in real consumption of non-farm households caused by higher food prices seems to have been only partly offset by increased spending by farmers. There also seems to have been a sizeable shift of income between consumers and some basic industries, whose profits increased sharply. Profits in the petroleum industry, for example, almost doubled in 1974, with after-tax income increasing by $6 billion over the previous year. The chemical and steel industries also registered a sharp rise in profits, though on a smaller scale. The net effect of these shifts seems to have been deflationary, since the increase in investment in these industries remained significantly below the increase in profits.

It is more difficult to say whether inflation has exerted a dampening influence on demand by reducing household spending propensities. Some econometric studies suggest that unanticipated inflation raises the savings ratio of households, in reaction to uncertainty as to future real incomes [5]. The continued rise in the savings ratio through 1973 can be interpreted as evidence in this regard. However, the behaviour of this ratio was very erratic in 1974 and early 1975 (Diagram 5). Consumer reactions to the energy crisis and the precipitant deterioration of employment conditions seem to offer a better explanation of the weakening of consumption.

(c) *Policy effects*

Contractionary monetary and fiscal policy effects, both intended and unintended ones, have probably played a very important role in pushing the economy into recession. Demand management policies were progressively tightened during most of 1973. Following the outbreak of the oil crisis, the Administration was faced with both a sharp decline in demand and a steep trend of inflation. As the decline in demand was up to the summer at least viewed as a temporary effect of the oil crisis, the fight against inflation was considered to be the most important task. Consequently, it was intended that policy remain relatively restrictive, though not so severe as to prevent the expected moderate recovery. The budget proposed

5 See F. Juster and P. Wachtel, " Inflation and the Consumer ", *Brookings Papers on Economic Activity* (N° 1, 1973) and " A Note Inflation and the Savings Ratio ", (N° 3, 1972).

in February for fiscal year 1975 (1st July, 1974 to 30th June, 1975) reflected this stance. With a rise of 11 per cent in expenditures and a somewhat slower growth in projected revenues, mainly reflecting weaker economic conditions, the unified federal budget would show a deficit increasing from $4.7 billion in FY1974 to $9.4 billion in FY1975 ; the corresponding calendar year balance would swing from a surplus of $0.6 billion to a deficit of $4.6 billion (on national income accounts basis). However, the full employment budget, which attempts to exclude the effects of changes in the level of economic activity on expenditure and revenue, was expected to register a slight surplus in 1974 as in 1973. Because of the unexpected severity of inflation this general stance was not changed in the course of the year in spite of continued weak demand. An Administration programme combining some tax relief for lower income families with higher taxes for upper income families was proposed in October after the « summit meetings »[6] but did not pass Congress. A decisive shift toward expansionary fiscal policy with a major tax cut (discussed in detail in Part II) took place only after the sharp deterioration of the economy in the fourth quarter.

Though the intended fiscal policy stance was one of only moderate restraint, the actual fiscal impact was severely restrictive. During previous recessions the federal budget exerted a considerable automatic stabilizing effect, as the deceleration or decline in personal incomes resulted in a lower average tax burden (Table 6). However, this stabilizing effect tends to be offset if inflation remains high or accelerates, thereby pushing individuals into higher tax brackets. Indeed, average tax rates increased by 0.7 percentage point between 1973 and 1974, whereas in the previous three recessions there was an average fall of 0.2 percentage point[7]. Inflation also distorted corporate taxes. Increases in materials prices led to large inventory profits for most firms, even though real cash flows were stagnant or falling. Consequently, corporate taxes rose by $1.3 billion from the third quarter of 1973 to the third quarter of 1974 while profits after inventory valuation adjustment were nearly unchanged, which meant a considerable deterioration of business financial positions. Depreciation allowances based on purchase costs fell further and further behind actual replacement costs, thus also resulting in an overstatement of profits and heightened tax liabilities. Though budget expenditures rose during 1974, most of the increases were confined to transfer payments, largely a consequence of the recession itself. The net result was that the actual budget remained almost in balance through most of 1974, in spite of the deterioration of economic activity (Table 7). This implies that inflation-induced fiscal drag totally offset the built-in stabilizer effect of the budget. While the full employment budget tends to be distorted by high and variable rates of inflation, nevertheless the large swing from deficit to surplus up to the third quarter of 1974 suggests that important restrictive effects resulted from the federal budget during the early part of the recession.

The restrictive budget influences were strongly reinforced by the adoption of a particularly tight monetary policy stance from March through July 1974. The primary objective following an earlier effort (December 1973 through February 1974) to stimulate aggregate demand was to dampen monetary growth in order to combat the marked acceleration in the advance of prices. However, because of the effect of inflation and speculative inventory accumulation in supporting business credit demands and because of a very strong rise in foreign demands for bank credit associated with the rise in oil import values, monetary growth remained

---

6 These summit meetings consisted of a convocation of leading economists and public and private authorities for an open discussion of the current state of the economy and appropriate policies.

7 A similar decline in " effective tax rates " in 1974 would have meant a reduction of personal income taxes of some $ 10 billion.

Table 6   **Effective Tax Rates on Individual Income**

Calendar Year	Taxable personal income ($ bill.)	Individual tax liability ($ bill.)	Effective tax rate (%)
1950	212	18.4	8.7
1951	242	24.2	10.0
1952	258	27.8	10.8
1953	272	29.4	10.8
1954*	272	26.7	9.8
1955	292	29.6	10.1
1956	312	32.7	10.5
1957	327	34.4	10.5
1958*	332	34.3	10.3
1959	354	38.6	10.9
1960*	370	39.5	10.7
1961	381	42.2	11.1
1962	406	44.9	11.1
1963	427	48.2	11.3
1964	457	47.2	10.3
1965	494	49.6	10.0
1966	540	56.1	10.4
1967	576	63.0	10.9
1968	627	71.5[1]	11.4
1969	683	78.9[1]	11.6
1970*	725	81.9[1]	11.3
1971	765	85.4	11.2
1972	834	93.6	11.2
1973	934	107.0	11.5
1974*	1 007	122.4[2]	12.2

1   Excluding surcharge.
2   Before tax rebate.
*   Years of recession.
Source: Direct Communication to the OECD.

relatively strong throughout the first half of the year.   By July the unusual growth in credit demands, coupled with the general malaise resulting from the then emerging troubles of Franklin National Bank and the collapse of the Herstatt Bank in Germany, produced historically high interest rates and considerable dislocations in financial markets (Diagram 10).   The most severely hit was the mortgage market, as a substantial outflow of funds from thrift institutions took place in the summer months.   Utility companies and state and local governments also found it difficult to issue new bonds.   After mid-July, the combined effect of the tight monetary policy and the induced falling level of real economic activity began to produce a deceleration of monetary growth and a decline of short-term interest rates.   Though the growth rate of the money stock fell below the range of official target values in August, monetary policy remained essentially passive until September because of conflicting concerns about the persistence of inflation and the severe pressures which had characterised financial markets in mid-summer.

Since September, when most inflation indexes peaked, the Federal Reserve has pursued a more active policy to drive interest rates down and monetary growth up.   By that time, however, the cumulative downswing of demand had already gathered so much momentum that the easier monetary policy stance failed to reverse the recessionary tendencies.   The most important instrumental action taken to achieve the higher money supply growth objectives has been an expansionary open-market policy under which the Federal Reserve has injected sufficient

Table 7 Budgets of the Public Sector

$ billion annual rates (National Income Account Basis)

	1971	1972	1973	1974	1973 Q.1	Q.2	Q.3	Q.4	1974 Q.1	Q.2	Q.3	Q.4	1975 Q.1
Federal Government:													
Actual													
Receipts	198.5	227.2	258.5	291.1	249.1	255.0	261.8	268.3	278.1	288.6	302.8	294.7	283.8
Expenditures	220.3	244.7	264.2	299.1	260.2	262.4	263.4	270.6	281.0	291.6	304.7	319.3	338.5
Balance	−21.9	−17.5	−5.6	−8.1	−11.2	−7.4	−1.7	−2.3	−2.8	−3.0	−1.9	−24.5	−54.7
Full-employment													
Receipts	216.4	232.4	265.9	319.9	253.8	261.2	270.2	278.3	296.1	312.9	333.0	337.2	
Expenditures	217.9	242.7	263.1	296.5	258.9	261.2	262.5	269.7	279.4	290.1	302.6	315.4	
Balance	−1.5	−10.3	2.8	23.4	−5.1	−0.1	7.7	8.6	16.6	22.9	30.4	21.8	
State and local Government:													
Actual													
Receipts	152.2	177.2	193.5	207.7	190.3	192.0	194.6	197.3	200.6	205.3	210.9	213.9	219.8
Expenditures	148.8	164.9	184.4	205.9	177.0	181.7	186.2	192.7	197.4	203.3	208.8	214.0	221.5
Balance	3.4	12.3	9.2	1.8	13.2	10.4	8.4	4.6	3.2	2.0	2.1	−0.1	−1.7
(excluding social insurance funds)			(0.1)	(−7.9)			(−0.8)	(−4.7)	(−6.4)	(−7.7)	(−7.7)	(−9.9)	(−11.6)

Sources: Department of Commerce, *Survey of Current Business*, and Council of Economic Advisors, *Economic Report of the President*, 1975.

funds into the money market to provide for a high rate of growth in currency and
bank reserves and to enable money-market instruments, notably Federal funds,
to trade at gradually declining yields. In addition, reserve requirements against
bank deposits have been cut on three occasions from September through January
amounting to a reduction of approximately 6 per cent in overall requirements.

Diagram 9   **Monetary Variables: Targets and Results**

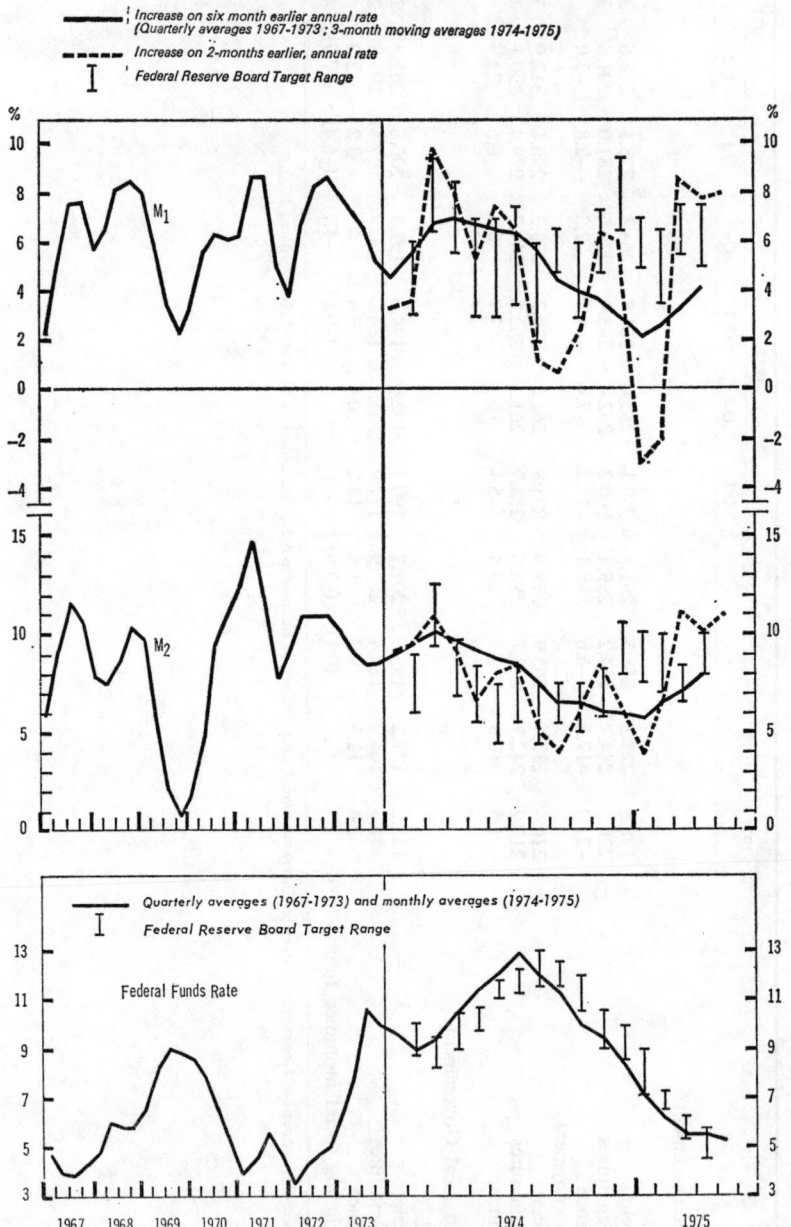

NOTE : Targets are Those agreed on by The Federal Reserve for periods comprizing the
current and follouding month.

Source: Federal Reserve Board, *Federal Reserve Bulletin.*

Diagram 10 Interest Rates

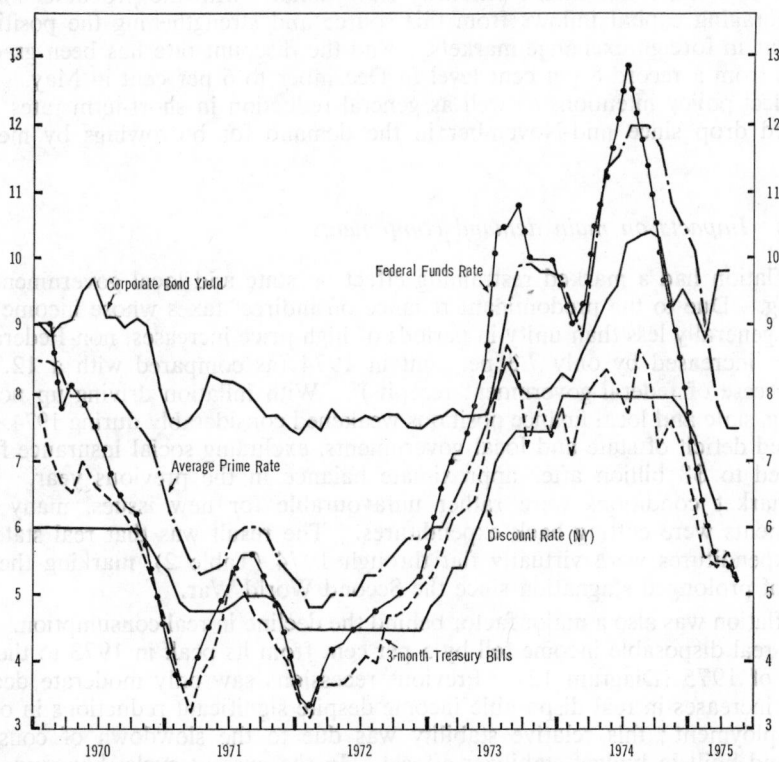

Source: Federal Reserve Board, *Federal Reserve Bulletin* and Dept. of Commerce, *Business Conditions Digest.*

Diagram 11 Deviations from Trend: Real Money Stock and GNP

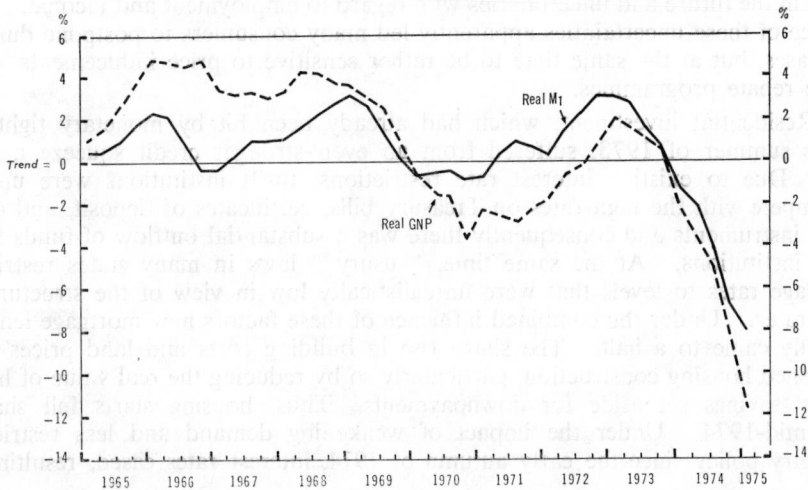

NOTE Trend calculations are for 1960-1974. M_1 is deflated by the implicit GNP deflator.
Source: Dept. of Commerce, *Survey of Current Business.*

In April, the Board of Governors cut reserve requirements on foreign borrowings of member commercial banks, primarily Euro-dollars, with the probable intention of encouraging capital inflows from this source and strengthening the position of the dollar in foreign exchange markets. And the discount rate has been gradually reduced from a record 8 per cent level in December to 6 per cent in May. These cuts reflect policy intentions as well as general reduction in short-term rates and a sustained drop since mid-November in the demand for borrowings by member banks.

(d)   Impacts on main demand components

Inflation had a marked restraining effect on state and local government real spending. Due to the predominant reliance on indirect taxes whose income elasticity is generally less than unity in periods of high price increases, non-Federal tax revenues increased by only 7.3 per cent in 1974 (as compared with a 12.7 per cent increase of federal government receipts)[8]. With inflation driving up nominal spending, state and local finance positions weakened considerably during 1974. The combined deficit of state and local governments, excluding social insurance funds, amounted to $8 billion after approximate balance in the previous year. Since bond market conditions were rather unfavourable for new issues, many local governments were cutting back expenditures. The result was that real state and local expenditures were virtually flat through 1974 (Table 2), marking the first period of prolonged stagnation since the Second World War.

Inflation was also a major factor behind the decline in real consumption. The level of real disposable income fell by 5 per cent from its peak in 1973 to the first quarter of 1975 (Diagram 12). Previous recessions saw only moderate declines or even increases in real disposable income despite significant reductions in output and employment ; this relative stability was due to the slowdown of consumer prices and built-in budget stabilizer effects. In the current cycle, however, wage increases, though sizeable, lagged far behind consumer prices and, as noted above, fiscal drag actually tended to reduce disposable income during the greater part of 1974. The weakness of consumption, as well as its erratic pattern, may also have been strongly influenced by the sentiment of consumers, jolted by the oil crisis and torn between the conflicting incentives of expectations of even higher prices in the future and uncertainties with regard to employment and income. The balance of these uncertainties apparently led many consumers to postpone durable purchases, but at the same time to be rather sensitive to price inducements, such as the rebate programmes.

Residential investment, which had already been hit by monetary tightness in the summer of 1973, suffered from an even stronger credit squeeze a year later. Due to existing interest rate restrictions, thrift institutions were unable to compete with the high rates on Treasury bills, certificates of deposit, and other credit instruments and consequently there was a substantial outflow of funds from those institutions. At the same time, " usury " laws in many states restricted mortgage rates to levels that were unrealistically low in view of the structure of other rates. Under the combined influence of these factors new mortgage lending virtually came to a halt. The sharp rise in building costs and land prices also dampened housing construction, particularly so by reducing the real value of home buyers' savings set aside for downpayments. Thus, housing starts fell sharply after mid-1974. Under the impact of weakening demand and less restrictive monetary policy since the early autumn of 1974, interest rates eased, resulting in

---

8   Excluding federal grants-in-aid, indirect taxes account for two-thirds of state and local revenue. Real estate and specific duty taxes in particular tend to lag the price rise.

Diagram 12 **Cyclical Comparisons of Disposable Income**

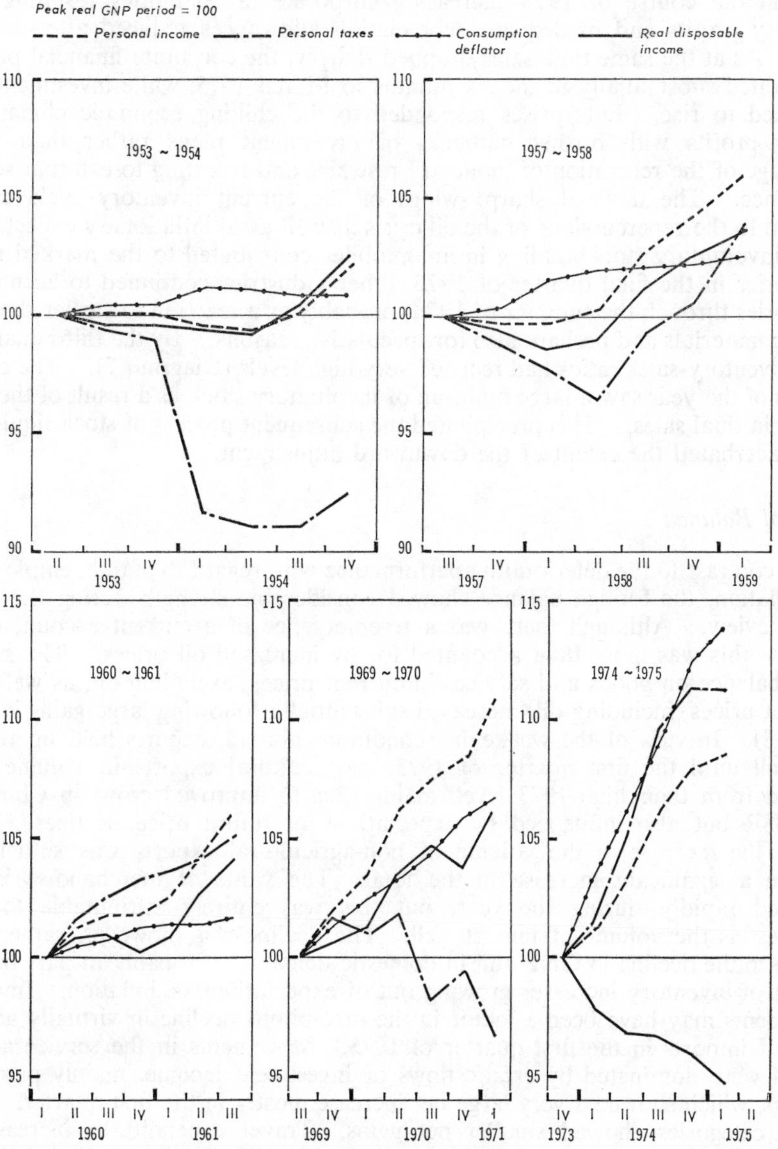

Peak real GNP period = 100

- - - - Personal income ▬·▬·▬ Personal taxes ●▬●▬● Consumption deflator ▬▬▬ Real disposable income

Source: Dept. of Commerce, *Survey of Current Business.*

renewed flows of funds to the thrift institutions in the fourth quarter. Nevertheless, until very recently housing starts remained depressed, in contrast to the experience of previous recessions, when starts responded very quickly. A sizeable overhang of unsold houses and sharp increases in unemployment appear to have been the most important reason for the continued weakness in the housing market.

The direct impact of inflation and the other special recession factors on business investment is less clear-cut and hence more difficult to assess. The commodity boom, the energy crisis and the related price explosions and improved medium-term prospects have importantly stimulated investment demand in a number of industries, such as petroleum, chemicals and paper. On the other hand, in the course of 1974 increasing corporate tax liabilities resulting from inventory profits and inadequate depreciation allowances reduced after-tax cash flows. As at the same time sales dropped sharply, the corporate financial position deteriorated substantially in the six months to March 1975, while investment costs continued to rise. Enterprises responded to the chilling economic climate and sagging profits with further cutbacks of investment plans rather than taking advantage of the relaxation of monetary restraint and resorting to external sources of finance. The unusual sharp swings of the current inventory cycle can be ascribed to the repercussions of the oil crisis as well as to inflationary expectations. While involuntary stockbuilding in automobiles contributed to the marked rise in inventories in the final quarter of 1973, other industries continued to accumulate inventories through the summer of 1974, probably as a reaction to earlier shortages of basic materials and perhaps also for speculative reasons. By the third quarter of 1974 inventory-sales ratios had reached very high levels (Diagram 7). The closing months of the year saw a large build-up of involuntary stock as a result of the steep decline in final sales. This precipitated the subsequent process of stock liquidation and exacerbated the extent of the downward adjustment.

External Balance

In contrast to the deteriorating performance with regard to output, employment, and inflation, the foreign balance showed considerable strength during the period under review. Although there was a re-emergence of a current account deficit in 1974, this was more than accounted for by increased oil prices. The surplus in the balance on goods and services in current prices, excluding oil, as well as in constant prices, including oil, increased substantially following large gains in 1973 (Table 8). In view of the weakening conditions abroad, exports held up remarkably well until the first quarter of 1975. Agricultural exports in volume terms declined from their high 1973 level, mainly due to improved crops in China and the USSR but also influenced by expectations of future price declines. Nevertheless, the increase in the volume of non-agricultural exports was sufficient to produce a significant increase in the total. The value of merchandise imports increased rapidly during the year, but this was entirely attributable to price increases, as the volume of imports fell. The decline was, however, rather small relative to the decline in GNP and in domestic demand. Probably in part this was a result of inventory increases growing out of expectations of inflation. Inventory adjustments may have been a factor in the precipitous decline in virtually all categories of imports in the first quarter of 1975. Movements in the service account in 1974 were dominated by erratic flows of investment income, mainly petroleum earnings, which showed a very large net increase mostly in the first quarter. Other service categories showed smaller net gains. Travel expenditures increased by less than 4 per cent (as opposed to a 14 per cent increase in receipts) indicating a considerable decline in real terms. The result was that the rise in net invisibles earnings largely offset the larger trade deficit. Consequently, in spite of the enormous expansion of oil import costs, the current account deficit was rather minor, the equivalent of about 1 per cent of GNP, relatively much less than in most OECD countries[9].

Thus 1974 represents a continuation of the marked turnaround in the foreign balance. After many years of losses, US export market shares showed a further

---

9 It should be noted that the current account figure presented here does not include the extraordinary Indian Rupee debt cancellation, which in the official figures was registered as a government transfer but which was fully offset in the capital account and did not represent any foreign exchange outflow.

Table 8 **Exports and Imports**
$ billion

	Current Prices					1958 Prices				
	1970	1971	1972	1973	1974	1970	1971	1972	1973	1974
Exports, merchandise	42.5	43.3	49.4	71.4	98.3	33.9	33.5	37.1	45.8	49.6
Agriculture	7.3	7.8	9.5	18.0	22.4	..	..	7.8	9.9	9.0
Non-agriculture	35.1	35.5	39.9	53.4	75.9	..	..	29.3	35.8	40.7
Services[1]	19.9	22.2	23.2	30.7	46.1	18.3	18.7	18.6	20.8	22.3
Income on investments	8.6	9.5	10.2	14.0	26.1					
Total exports, goods and services	62.4	65.5	72.6	102.1	144.4	52.2	52.2	55.7	66.6	71.9
Imports, merchandise	39.9	45.6	55.8	70.4	103.8	34.2	37.2	42.3	45.3	44.6
Fuels	3.2	4.0	5.1	8.9	27.4	..	..	4.4	6.0	5.6
Non-fuels	36.7	41.6	50.7	61.5	76.4	..	..	37.9	39.4	38.7
Services[1]	19.6	20.2	22.7	27.5	37.0	15.8	15.4	16.4	16.7	18.3
Payments on investments	5.1	4.8	5.8	8.8	15.9					
Total imports, goods and services	59.5	65.8	78.5	97.9	140.8	50.0	52.6	58.7	62.0	62.9
Net exports, goods and services	2.9	-.3	-5.9	4.2	3.6	2.2	-.4	-3.0	4.6	9.0
Excluding fuels	6.1	3.7	-.8	13.1	31.0					

1 Includes military transactions.
Source: Department of Commerce, *Survey of Current Business.*

Diagram 13 **Exports, Imports and Trade Balance**
Quarterly averages of monthly figures

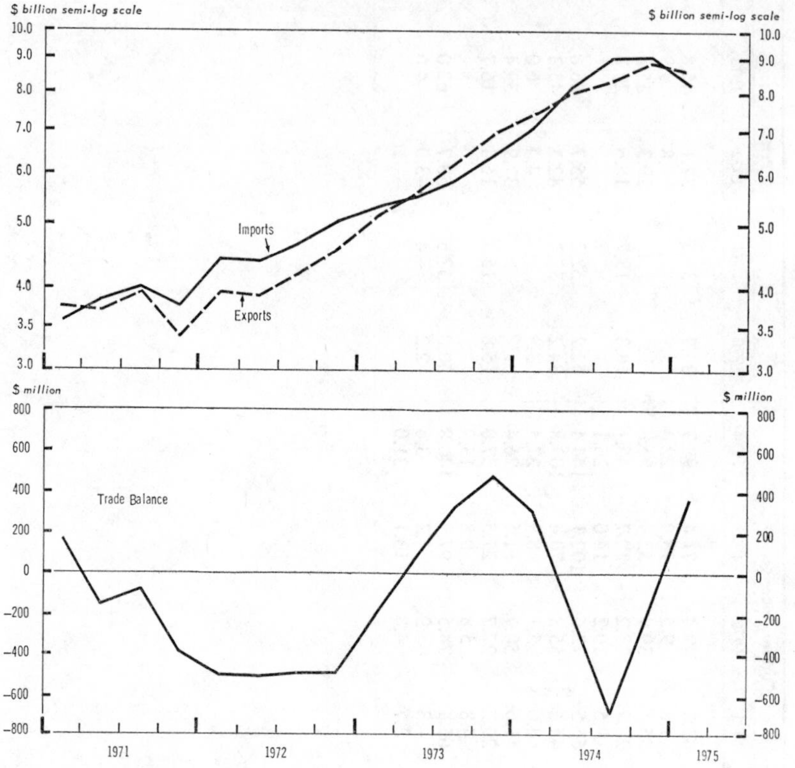

Source: OECD, *Main Economic Indicators.*

increase on the strong advances of 1973.   As opposed to 1973, these gains cannot be attributed to the special factors which led to the large volume of agricultural exports.   Export increases were broadly based geographically (Table 9) ; sales to most areas increased more rapidly than those of the other large OECD countries except — as in the case of the Sino-Soviet countries — where agricultural exports were particularly important in 1973[10].   Though imports increased as a share of domestic demand, it may well be that the inventory accumulations were mainly responsible, as this share declined very considerably in the first quarter of 1975. The depressed situation in the US economy certainly reduced imports and perhaps contributed somewhat to exports, as delivery times undoubtedly shortened and some enterprises may have given more attention to export markets.   Exports of course were also affected by the weakening markets abroad, but as US domestic demand was at a cyclically lower position relative to her main trading partners there probably was some benefit to the net balance. Furthermore, the composition of US exports magnified the cyclical element of strength in 1974 ; capital goods, which have a heavy weight in the export total, were aided by the relatively high backlogs of orders while consumer goods, more substantial in the import bill,

10   The value of US exports to the OPEC countries increased by over 85 per cent in 1974 and accounted for 11 per cent of the total increase in exports.

were affected by the early downswing in personal consumption. However, cyclical factors probably accounted for less than half of the marked improvement of net exports in real terms and the more than doubling of the non-oil balance in value terms[11]. Sharply higher agricultural prices accounted for much of the value improvement, but the value and volume increases in manufactured goods exports were even more important (Table 8). Price controls may have added to exports in 1973 (as some basic products were diverted abroad), but this probably did not occur to any important degree in 1974. Probably an important factor in the strengthening foreign balance was the cumulative effect of the sharp decline in relative export prices, which in turn was closely connected with the falling effective dollar exchange rate (Diagram 14). These relative price reductions have greatly expanded the range of products in which US suppliers are competitive[12].

A major feature of the capital account was the greatly increased importance of US capital markets in the financing of the foreign exchange requirements of other countries resulting from their higher oil bills. While the relatively small US current account deficit involved no important financing requirements, the oil

Table 9 **Export Performance**
Per cent increases in value

	United States				Other major OECD Countries[1]			
	Av. 71-72 / 61-62	72 / 71	73 / 72	74 / 73	Av. 71-72 / 61-62	72 / 71	73 / 72	74 / 73
Total	8.2	12.6	43.6	38.1	12.6	18.8	35.0	33.5
Manufactured goods	9.3	10.4	31.9	42.0	13.2	18.9	33.6	34.4[2]
Non-manufactured goods	5.9	18.2	72.3	30.9	10.6	18.2	40.9	34.2[2]
to:								
OECD	9.0	13.2	38.1	33.2	13.5	20.7	34.1	27.3
N. America	11.2	19.8	21.4	32.3	14.8	17.1	17.7	27.5
Oceania	8.5	−11.7	69.9	55.3	7.2	−0.4	42.5	58.8
Japan	10.2	21.9	68.2	28.4	13.6	23.4	76.4	19.4
Europe	7.3	7.9	39.7	34.0	13.3	22.8	38.7	26.6
non-OECD	6.9	11.2	50.8	49.1	10.4	12.7	38.2	52.7
Sino-Soviet	17.5	128.1	183.6	−9.7	12.9	27.7	47.4	52.2
OPEC	8.6	17.8	31.0	85.5	10.4	24.7	40.6	74.8
Other Latin America	5.9	13.5	42.2	57.4	8.9	16.6	27.5	68.4
South East Asia	9.1	16.5	58.2	38.2	14.4	10.0	45.8	36.9
Relatively developed primary producing countries	9.5	−11.8	46.4	39.0	12.8	−0.4	40.4	45.2
Other developing countries	3.1	−8.8	36.4	48.8	7.9	2.8	29.0	41.5

1 Includes Canada, Belgium, France, W. Germany, Italy, Japan, Netherlands and UK.
2 Excludes Italy.
Source: OECD Secretariat.

11 OECD trade model calculations, designed to provide some idea of orders of magnitude, indicate that the cyclical position of the US economy (relative to her trading partners) might have resulted in a level of imports $ 5 billion less than at capacity growth. At the same time, the cyclical position of her main trading partners might have meant a $ 3 billion loss in exports, implying a net gain on the trade balance of $ 2 billion. As services would also be affected by the relatively lower cyclical position of the US, the net effect on the balance of goods and services would be somewhat larger.
12 The largest volume export increases were in the highly manufactured goods many of which have greater price elasticity: on the basis of value figures it appears that a wide variety of individual products were involved in the large increases.

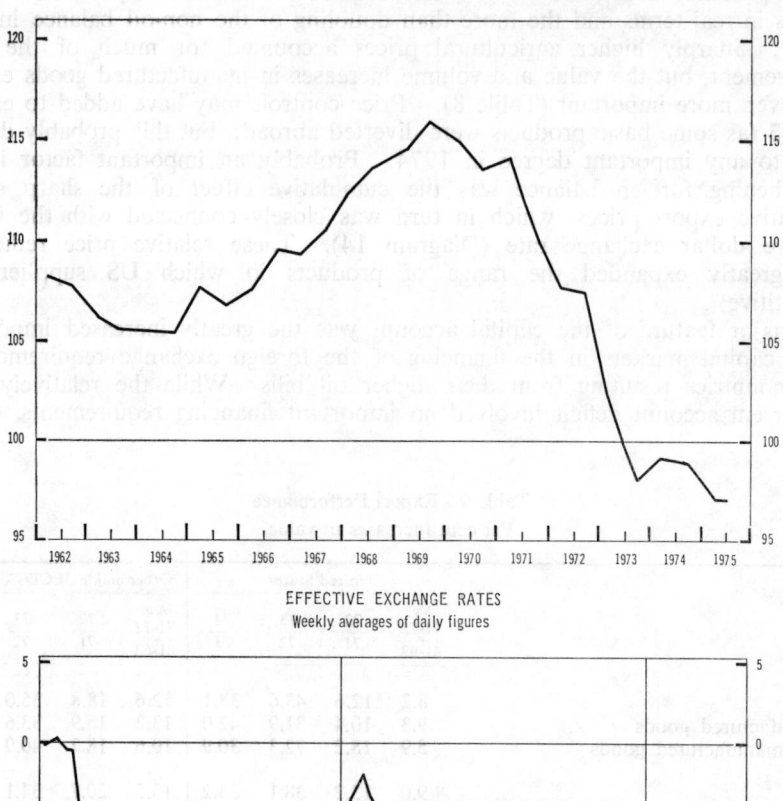

Diagram 14 **Relative Export Prices of Manufactures**
1973 = 100

EFFECTIVE EXCHANGE RATES
Weekly averages of daily figures

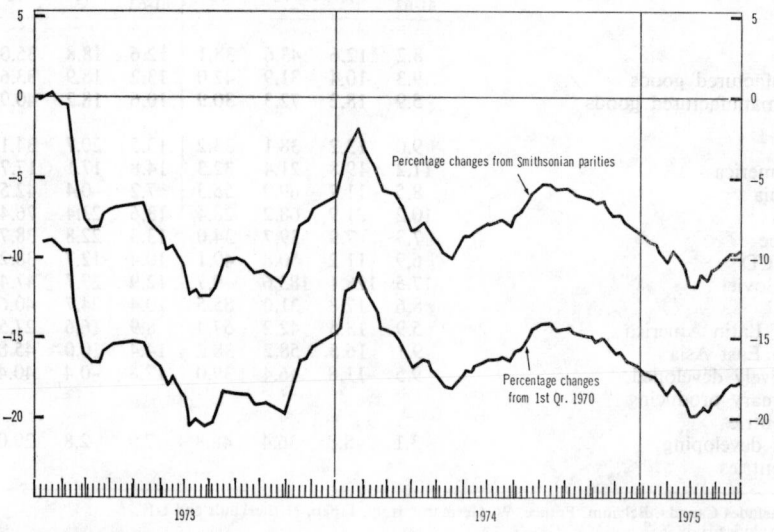

Percentage changes from Smithsonian parities

Percentage changes
from 1st Qr. 1970

Source: OECD Secretariat.

price increase greatly magnified the gross deficits (and surpluses) in the foreign accounts of the economies of the world. Consequently, there was a vastly increased need for balance of payments financing. Given the size and diversity of the US capital markets, it is not surprising that they played a substantial role in meeting the financing needs among many other countries. At the same time, there was an important inflow of foreign capital, including about $11¼ billion of direct investments in US markets out of the approximately $60 billion surplus in

Table 10 Balance of Payments

OECD Basis, Seasonally adjusted annual rate, $ billion

	1972	1973	1974	1973 Q.1	1973 Q.2	1973 Q.3	1973 Q.4	1974 Q.1	1974 Q.2	1974 Q.3	1974 Q.4	1975 Q.1
A CURRENT ACCOUNT												
Exports, fob[1]	49.4	71.4	98.3	61.7	67.8	73.8	82.2	89.8	96.8	100.1	106.3	108.9
Imports, fob	55.8	70.4	103.8	65.3	68.8	70.9	76.7	90.6	103.0	109.5	112.1	101.5
Trade balance	-6.4	1.0	-5.5	-3.6	-.9	2.9	5.5	-.8	-6.1	-9.4	-5.8	7.4
Services, net[2]	.5	3.2	9.1	2.2	1.6	3.4	5.7	12.4	6.1	9.4	9.5	6.1
Balance on goods and services	-5.9	4.2	3.6	-1.4	.7	6.2	11.3	11.6	0	-1.0	3.7	13.4
Private transfers, net	-1.0	-1.2	-1.0	-.9	-.9	-.9	-2.2	-1.1	-1.1	-1.0	-1.0	-1.0
Official transfers, net	-2.7	-2.6	-3.4	-2.1	-3.2	-2.7	-2.5	-2.8	-3.4	-4.0	-3.4	-3.8
Current balance	-9.7	.3	-.9	-4.5	-3.4	2.6	6.6	7.8	-4.5	-6.1	-.7	8.6
B CAPITAL ACCOUNT												
Long-term private capital	-.2	.1	-8.0	.3	-1.4	6.3	-4.6	.3	-4.6	8.4	-19.2	-7.0
Long-term official capital[2]	-1.3	-1.7	-2.1	-1.8	-.2	-1.2	-3.6	-1.6	-.5	.1	-6.4	-3.5
Basic balance	-11.2	-1.3	-10.9	-6.0	-5.0	7.7	-1.7	6.5	-9.5	-14.4	-26.3	-1.9
Non-monetary short-term private capital	-.6	-1.1	-.9	1.9	-.8	-1.0	-.8	-5.5	.3	2.6	-1.1	.5
Errors and omissions	1.9	-2.4	4.8	-15.5	3.5	-.6	2.9	4.3	5.7	4.6	4.7	7.4
Balance on non-monetary Transactions	-13.7	-4.8	-7.0	-23.5	-2.4	6.1	.4	5.4	-3.5	-7.1	-22.6	5.9
Private monetary institutions	2.5	-.8	-1.4	-19.5	3.9	3.2	9.4	-3.2	-13.2	7.6	3.2	-18.8
Short-term capital												
Assets	-2.2	-5.0	-18.2	-11.3	-1.6	-.8	-6.5	-20.6	-26.5	-9.4	-16.1	-12.7
Liabilities	4.7	4.3	16.8	-8.2	5.5	4.0	15.8	17.5	13.3	17.0	19.4	-6.2
Balance on official settlements	-11.2	-5.6	-8.4	-43.0	1.5	9.3	9.8	2.2	-16.8	.5	-19.4	-12.9
Liabilities to foreign official agencies	10.3	5.1	9.8	39.9	-1.2	-7.7	-10.6	-1.2	18.4	3.6	18.8	14.0
OPEC	.6	.4	9.9	:	:	:	:	4.0	9.6	15.6	10.8	.8
Other	9.7	4.7	-.2	:	:	:	:	-5.2	8.8	-12.0	8.0	13.2
Change in Reserves (+ = increase)	-.0	-.2	1.4	-.9	-.1	.1	.1	.8	1.4	4.0	-.5	1.3
Memorandum Item:												
Claims on foreigners reported by US banks	3.8	6.0	18.8	-11.9	-3.0	1.2	10.0	21.1	30.0	6.6	17.6	:
Liabilities to foreigners reported by US banks[3]	:	8.8	20.9	:	:	:	:	17.5	22.5	28.0	15.7	:
of which: OPEC	:	.5	4.0	:	:	:	:	2.5	4.4	7.4	1.5	:

1 Excluding military.
2 Excludes certain special transactions, notably the Indian Rupee debt cancellation.
3 Excludes government securities.

Sources: US Department of Commerce. *Survey of Current Business,* Federal Reserve Board, *Federal Reserve Bulletin* and OECD Secretariat.

the OPEC current account, almost all of it in rather liquid financial assets[13]. Obviously, however, the OPEC investment in assets in European markets, likewise mainly liquid, induced large additional flows to the US markets; short-term bank reported inflows from Switzerland, for example, amounted to over $6.6 billion, as compared to $0.5 billion in 1973. The total increase in liquid liabilities was almost $25 billion in 1974, as compared to an increase of $8.7 billion in 1973. At the same time there was a much larger demand for loan funds, particularly from Japan and Latin America, much of which was closely related to the financing of actual and anticipated deficits. As a result there was an unparalleled expansion of both bank claims and assets, primarily short-term (Table 10).

Besides the outflow through bank lending, there were large increases in direct investments abroad. With the revocation of restrictions on capital exports in January 1974 many enterprises transferred funds abroad rather than raising capital through security sales in European markets. Largely, as a result of rising US interest rates, the balance of the capital and current account flows raised the effective exchange rate of the dollar up to a level slightly above that of the end of 1973, before the erratic movements connected with the oil embargo. In the final portion of the year, however, the decline in US interest rates brought increased sales of foreign securities in US markets and a major reduction of capital inflows through the banking system. This, along with a considerable shift from inflows to outflows in the accounts of the petroleum companies, resulted in downward pressures on the dollar, in spite of the rapidly improving trade balance. Support operations, though substantial in the fourth quarter, were not sufficient to prevent a depreciation which started being reversed only in the second quarter of 1975.

II PROSPECTS

The Present Policy Stance

Given the severe and unexpected deterioration of the economic situation and the reduction of inflation, the fiscal policy stance changed dramatically early this year, with priority turning from price stabilisation to halting the decline in output and employment. In January, the Administration announced a package of tax cuts totalling $16 billion, together with energy conservation programmes. In the course of examination by Congress the bill was modified and the tax cut increased to $23 billion. The most important components of the tax measures are an $8.1 billion rebate for 1974 personal income taxes and a $7.8 billion reduction of withholding taxes (involving standard and minimum deductions and a $30 tax credit). These, together with other, less important, measures will result in an increment to personal income of roughly $20 billion for the year, about 2 per cent of disposable income[14]. For corporations an increase in the investment tax credit from 7 to 10 per cent is the major single item (for details see Table 11). Though the present bill will expire at the end of 1975, it is generally assumed (including in the present forecast) that the reduced tax schedules will be extended

---

13 Long-term investment in the private sector was probably about three-quarters of a billion dollars, with only minor sums going into direct investment. The bulk of OPEC funds was divided between government securities and bank and money market instruments. Increases in assets held in US banks are shown in the memorandum item in Table 9. Increases in all *officially* held OPEC liquid assets, comprising government securities as well as bank assets, would be included in " liquid liabilities to foreign official agencies ".

14 This compares with the 1964 tax cut, which added about 1.5 per cent to disposable income.

into 1976. Because of the one-time tax rebate in May, the impact of this programme will be particularly strong in the second quarter, when the tax reduction will reach $50 billion (annual rate) and disposable income will be boosted by about 5 per cent (Table 12). Thereafter, the fiscal impact will probably remain at an annual rate of about $14-15 billion through mid-1976. As no comprehensive energy programme appears imminent, the present forecast assumes that the $2 per barrel import duties on imported oil ($1 effective as of 1st February and a further $1 as of 1st June) will be maintained but incorporates no new measures for oil conservation[15].

Table 11   **Summary of 1975 Tax Cut Bill**
$ billion

Total	22.9
Tax reductions	22.8
Individual	18.5
1974 tax rebate	8.1
General tax credit[1]	5.3
Standard deductions increase[1]	2.5
Earned income credit[2]	1.5
New home purchase credit	0.6
Investment credit[3]	0.4
Child care	0.1
Corporate	4.3
Investment credit[3]	2.8
Surtax exemption and rate	1.5
Tax increases (corporate)	1.8
Percentage depletion	1.6
Foreign tax revisions	0.2
Expenditure increases	1.9
Bonus payment[4]	1.7
Extended unemployment	0.2

1 Reflects reduction of withholding tax schedules.
2 Consists of credit for taxpayers and for individuals who pay no taxes.
3 Effective for 1975 and 1976.
4 One-time payment of $ 50 to those eligible for social security benefits.
Source: Department of Commerce, *Survey of Current Business*, April 1975.

Combined with likely spending developments, the tax cut plan will probably result in a considerable net fiscal stimulus. The Administration has maintained a relatively cautious expenditure stance. The budget proposal made in February for Fiscal year 1976 projected an increase in federal expenditures from the previous year of 11.5 per cent to $349 billion. The proposals included considerable savings on appropriations for existing programmes and did not incorporate any new programmes. With a revenue figure of $297.5 billion, the initial estimate of the budget deficit on a unified basis amounted to $51.9 billion, compared with $34.6 billion in FY 1975. But with larger tax cuts and the higher expenditure ceiling recently adopted by Congress ($367 billion) the deficit may rise to around

15   It is presently estimated that the tariffs will increase taxes by about $ 5½ billion annually, with a marginal impact on incomes and prices.

Table 12 **Fiscal Impacts of Tax Cuts**
$ billion, annual rates

		1975		
	Q.1	Q.2	Q.3	Q.4
Personal taxes		−40.5	−11.8	−11.7
Corporate taxes	−1.8	−2.6	−2.9	−3.1
Personal transfers		−7.4		
Total change in federal deficit	−1.8	−50.5	−14.7	−14.8

Source: Bureau of Economic Analysis and Treasury Department.

$70 billion, about $4\frac{3}{4}$ per cent of GNP[16]. However much of the recent and prospective budget deficit is a reflection of the declining level of activity. Given the current programme, it appears that the full employment balance, intended to give a clearer idea of the discretionary element of fiscal policy, may move from a $23 billion surplus in calendar 1974 to $15 billion deficit in 1975 — the change representing 2 per cent of GNP — then swinging back to zero in the first half of 1976. Again the strongest impact is in the second quarter of 1975, when the full employment deficit may reach an annual rate of over $40 billion.

It is assumed that monetary policy will be essentially accommodating through 1975, though some tightening may occur in 1976. Money supply growth was very weak from the summer of 1974 through January 1975, in spite of a sharp decline in interest rates and a deliberate easing of monetary policy during the latter part of that period. In recent months, however, there has been some acceleration of monetary growth partly as a result of increased deficit spending financed by Federal Reserve and commercial bank purchases of Treasury securities. Interest rates continued to decline until late spring but have seen some rise thereafter. The Federal Reserve System recently (on 1st May) announced a set of target ranges for monetary aggregates covering the twelve months ending in March 1976 : 5-$7\frac{1}{2}$ per cent growth in the basic money stock. (M_1) with greater increase anticipated for broader aggregates M_2 and M_3 ($8\frac{1}{2}$-$10\frac{1}{2}$ and 10-12 per cent respectively). The M_1 target, viewed alone, does not appear to be consistent with an expansion of aggregate demand sufficient to reduce unemployment significantly within the forecast period, even allowing for some increase in velocity during the upswing. Strict adherence to this target combined with Treasury financing of a deficit of around $70 billion could well entail rising interest rates, particularly towards mid-1976 which in turn could slow down the expansion unduly. But the target rates for M_2 and M_3 are more supportive and the authorities have emphasized that the target objectives are flexible. In these circumstances, it is difficult to judge to what extent monetary policy will represent a constraint on the expansion. It is assumed here that monetary policy will not be operated so as to prevent a recovery of the size envisaged by the Secretariat.

Outlook

As noted, there are indications that the fall in activity is coming to an end. The long and sharp decline in housing starts was arrested in the first quarter and a sizeable pick-up was recorded in May. In recent two months employment regis-

16 The May revision of budget estimates by the Office Management and Budget shows a deficit of $ 60 billion for FY 1976, incorporating the tax cut and increases in expenditures approved by Congress. However, with further increases in expenditures expected, the deficit is likely to reach around $ 70 billion.

tered small increases and the fall in industrial production slowed considerably. Moreover, the improvement in two important leading indicators — durable goods orders and the survey by the National Association of Purchasing Agents — may be possible early signs of an upturn in activity. The recovery in the second half of the year forecast by the Secretariat, however, is mainly based on three factors: the significant change in fiscal and monetary policies to stimulate demand and specifically the large tax cuts taking effect in the second quarter; the fact that hourly wage earnings are now rising faster than consumer prices, reversing the earlier decline in real wages; and the likelihood that inventory liquidation will become much more moderate in the second half of the year following the large adjustment in the first half. As usual, the timing and strength of the recovery are subject to great uncertainty, but in view of these factors it seems reasonable to expect a recovery of activity led by private consumption and residential construction as from the third quarter. On the assumptions adopted, real GNP may rise at annual rates of 6-6½ per cent in the third and fourth quarters, though the expansion may slow down somewhat in the first two quarters of next year as the policy stimulus diminishes (Table 13). With this pattern of expansion and a rapid productivity gain — characteristic of the early stage of a recovery — the increase in employment would be moderate, in view of a probable rapid lengthening of working hours. Unemployment is therefore unlikely to fall substantially during the forecast period, perhaps remaining above 8½ per cent in the middle of 1976.

Table 13 **OECD Forecasts**
Seasonally adjusted per cent changes at annual rates of demand components in constant 1958 prices

	1973	1974	1975	1974		1975		1976
				I	II	I	II	I
Private consumption	4.7	–2.3	¼	–3.5	–1.3	–2	6	4
Federal expenditure	–6.1	–1.4	2¼	.0	1.6	2¾	2	2¾
State and local expenditure	6.0	2.9	1	2.7	–.6	1¾	1½	2¼
Total government expenditure	.8	1.1	1½	1.9	.3	2	1½	1¼
Non-residential investment	12.8	–.4	–14½	1.8	–9.6	–19½	–9½	–1¼
Residential investment	–4.1	–27.1	–23	–30.3	–28.7	–38¼	28½	43¾
Gross private fixed investment	7.9	–7.3	–16½	–6.7	–13.9	–23¼	–3½	7
Final domestic demand	4.5	–2.5	–2	–3.1	–3.0	–4½	4	4
Inventory change[1]	.5	–.3	–2	–1.1	–.3	–4¾	1¾	1½
Total domestic demand	4.9	–2.7	–4	–4.1	–3.3	–9	5¾	5½
Exports	19.6	8.0	–6¼	16.7	–7.9	–7½	–1½	3¾
Imports	5.6	1.5	–10¾	8.0	–3.7	–21¼	6¼	8½
Net exports[1]	1.0	.5	¼	.7	–.4	1	–½	–¼
GNP	5.9	–2.1	–3¾	–3.4	–3.7	–8	5	5¼
GNP deflator	5.6	10.3	9	10.7	11.9	9¼	6	6

1 Change on an annual basis as a per cent of GNP of previous period.
NOTE: The present forecasts do not take into account the preliminary figures for the second quarter of 1975.
Sources: Department of Commerce, *Survey of Current Business* and OECD Secretariat.

Expectations of a recovery are based primarily on the prospects for a rather strong increase in personal consumption. The first quarter pickup in real consumer expenditure was largely attributable to a rise in auto sales spurred on by temporary rebates; sales fell following the suspension of the rebates but may have steadied or regained some ground recently. Purchases of non-durable goods have shown a more steady trend, rising slightly in real terms since the beginning of the year. The slower rate in consumer prices, combined with steady advances in wage rates, and the stabilisation of the employment situation point to a positive growth in real personal income in the near future. Consumers response to the tax cuts, and particularly the one-time tax rebate, is difficult to predict, but it seems reasonable to expected that the sharp increase in real disposable income will have a sizeable impact on spending. It is assumed that about one-half of the addition to personal income will be spent in the second half of the year, with the savings ratio declining from an abnormally high level attained in the second quarter. On these assumptions there would be a strong boost to real private consumption beginning in the third quarter of 1975. However, the stimulus of the tax rebate will phase out as consumption patterns adjust to the reduced taxes by early 1976. Furthermore, though it is assumed that the lower tax schedules will be maintained in 1976, monthly withholding tax payments will increase next January since tax payments in the last 8 months of 1975 will reflect tax reductions for the entire year. Consequently, real consumption may show some deceleration in 1976.

Residential construction, the demand component most severely affected by the current recession, also seems likely to stage a recovery in the near future. Housing starts, which typically lead the upswing in residential investment by one to two quarters stagnated at a very low level in the first quarter. Probably the large stock of unsold houses has been a considerable drag on the market. However, as the stock is reduced, the renewed inflows of funds to institutions specializing in housing finance and the fall in mortgage rates should permit a recovery. As noted, building permits have been rising recently, and housing starts picked up sharply in May. The rise in real wages and improved employment prospects should also help. However, the recovery may be more moderate than during most previous upswings, as construction costs have risen relative to the general price level, mortage rates, though falling, are still high by past standards, and unemployment is likely to remain high for some time to come.

Other elements of final demand will probably remain weak. Government expenditures may show only slight increases in real terms over the next year. Because of the prospect of a large budget deficit, Congress as well as the Administration may be cautious in launching new spending programmes. Available information suggests that increases in outlays will be devoted mainly to transfer payments, with real federal purchases of goods and services showing little growth. The deterioration of the financial position of states and local authorities may be arrested in the near future but their real expenditures are unlikely to show much strength.

Non-residential fixed investment is likely to remain depressed throughout the forecast period. Business investment normally lags behind in cyclical recoveries, and there is good reason to expect that lags will be longer in the current cycle. New orders for durable goods industries, despite the rise in April and May, are still at low levels in view of recent inflation. Business cash flows have deteriorated markedly in constant dollars and equity markets, despite the rise in stock prices in recent months, remain relatively weak. In spite of sharp declines since mid-1974, long-term interest rates are still high by historical standards and this is likely to be the case for some time to come. Indeed 1976 might see renewed upward pressures on interest rates. Perhaps most important, capacity utilisation rates are currently lower than during any of the previous post-war recessions. Consequently, the investment tax credit may not have any important impact on investment until 1976, when rising output provides more inducement to capacity expansion.

The liquidation of inventories is expected to continue through most of 1975, though at progressively lower rates. As a result of the exceedingly large inventory additions of the period from the fourth quarter of 1973 through the fourth quarter of 1974, the recent substantial reductions have probably not yet brought inventories, especially of non-auto durables, down to desired levels. Nevertheless, with the tapering off of inventory liquidation after mid-1975, stock movements will constitute a positive element in GNP formation during the forecast period.

Some further moderation of inflation may be expected in 1975, though a return to the relative price stability of the 1960's is not likely. With the sharp decreases in demand and pervasive excess inventories, wholesale prices, particularly of basic materials, declined through March. This is likely to show up in a further deceleration of consumer prices over the next few months. Based on current expectations of large agricultural harvests, food prices, in spite of recent increases, should show more stability than in 1974. However, wage increases will probably limit the slowdown in inflation. Under the impact of high unemployment, adjusted hourly earnings have recently decelerated approximately to a 7 per cent annual rate of increase. However, as labour strives to recoup real earnings little further moderation can be expected[17]. Recovery will bring strong initial increases in productivity and hence dampen unit labour costs, but this effect will diminish as the recovery proceeds. Also, the recent declines in material prices are not likely to continue once the upswing is firmly established. The same may be said of the presently widespread practices of price rebating and discounting. Consequently, the deceleration of prices may not persist into 1976.

Net exports in constant dollars will probably fall in the course of the forecast period. Given the generally better crop prospects in many important food importing countries agricultural exports are likely to decrease. Shipments of machinery and equipment, which weigh heavily in US exports, were relatively strong up to the first quarter, but may be weak in the coming period due to the continued weakness of investment activity in most countries. Imports, on the other hand, may turn up with the recovery of aggregate demand, especially since consumer goods weigh heavily in US imports. The decline in net exports may be somewhat sharper in current than in constant prices, as a mild adverse terms of trade movement is likely, due mainly to falling agricultural prices. Net service earnings can be expected to decline because of decreased profit flows from petroleum companies. While the current account of the balance of payments may show a surplus for 1975 as a whole, a small but widening deficit probably will appear beginning in the second half of the year.

III FINANCING THE FEDERAL BUDGET DEFICIT

The unusually large deficits now foreseen for the Federal budget in 1975 and 1976 have occasioned a lively discussion of the potential dangers for financial markets. Throughout the entire period from the end of World War II until the late 1960's, the Treasury was practically a by-stander in the capital markets, providing room for the personal, corporate, and municipal, sectors to accumulate debt at rapid rates and low costs (see Table 14). Even in the period of large Federal deficits from 1967 through 1972, growth in Federal government debt accounted for only 8 ½ per cent of total debt accumulation. But in 1975 and 1976, this ratio may reach 35 per cent or more. This will still be a long way from the depression and war years of 1930-45, when the Federal government more than accounted for all growth in debt in the United States ; nonetheless, the magnitudes clearly are large enough to warrant an inquiry as to whether the associated

---

17 As noted earlier, wage demands of organized labour have not abated, in spite of rising unemployment. Average first year wage increases in major settlements remained above 12 per cent in the first quarter of 1975. As 1976 is a heavy bargaining year, the trend of collective bargaining settlements over the next few quarters will be important indications as to the extent of cost push inflation in 1976.

Table 14   Accumulation of Debt, 1930-1975

	Federal Government		Other domestic sectors		Federal as % of total
	$ Billion Per year	Per cent of GNP	$ Billion Per year	Per cent of GNP	
1930-39	2.6	3.0	−3.8	−4.4	110.4
1940-45	35.0	21.1	1.6	1.0	
1946-66	0.9	0.2	38.6	8.9	2.3
1967-72	11.6	1.2	127.0	13.2	8.4
1973	7.9	0.6	219.7	17.0	3.5
1974	13.0	0.9	174.2	12.5	6.9
1975[1]	81	5½	153	10½	35

1 The tables in this chapter contain forecasts of changes in financial assets and liabilities for 1975 which have been estimated as being consistent with the expected developments in aggregate demand described in the preceding sections.

Sources: Council of Economic Advisers, Economic Report of the President 1975, Federal Reserve System, Flow of Funds Accounts, and Secretariat estimates.

financing requirement might be so great as to crowd other sectors out of the credit and capital markets.

Budget Deficits and the Economy

The Federal budget has in fact been in deficit continuously since 1970 (Diagram 15), though the reasons for and the magnitudes of the revenue shortfalls have varied. The restrictive fiscal policy stance which was initiated in 1968 had produced a temporary budget surplus in the following year as the growth of expenditure lagged the increase in receipts. But as the recession emerged in 1970, tax revenues declined and swung the government accounts into deficit. The subsequent policy reversal and consequent economic recovery reduced but did not eliminate this imbalance. Since the second half of 1973, a similar cycle, though much more pronounced, has unfolded. The hypothetical « high-employment » budget shifted into surplus by mid-1973, but the decline of aggregate demand below trend has prevented the achievement of an actual surplus. The economy is now entering a transitional phase in which the budget deficit must temporarily be considerably larger than in other recent years[18]. The downturn of the economy has continued in the first half of 1975 while fiscal policy has just started to move towards expansion, as will be reflected in a marked swing of the high-employment balance from surplus to deficit during 1975. As the private sectors of the economy are expected to revive in response to this shift and to the expansionary monetary policies pursued since last September, employment, income and the flow of tax receipts will be pushed up. As a result of this expansion and an anticipated rise in the high-employment balance following the distribution of the 1974 tax rebate, the borrowing requirements of the Administration should fall substantially and provide room for credit-financed private investment[19].

As the size of the Federal deficit rises this year and the Treasury goes more and more to the public to borrow the funds to cover the gap, it may have to offer

18 An important feature of the current recession appears to have been a simultaneous reduction in private investment and an increse in private savings not matched by additional credit-financed expenditure elsewhere (net exports or government real spending). In terms of financial equilibrium the deflationary demand gap can be seen as an excess margin of voluntary lending (desired financial asset formation) over domestic borrowing.

19 There is of course no guarantee that the deficit will ever disappear. The desirability or otherwise of maintaining a deficit of some size will depend on the strengh and the viability of the prospective upswing of private investment.

Diagram 15 Federal Budget Balances: Actual and High Employment
Negative figures are deficits

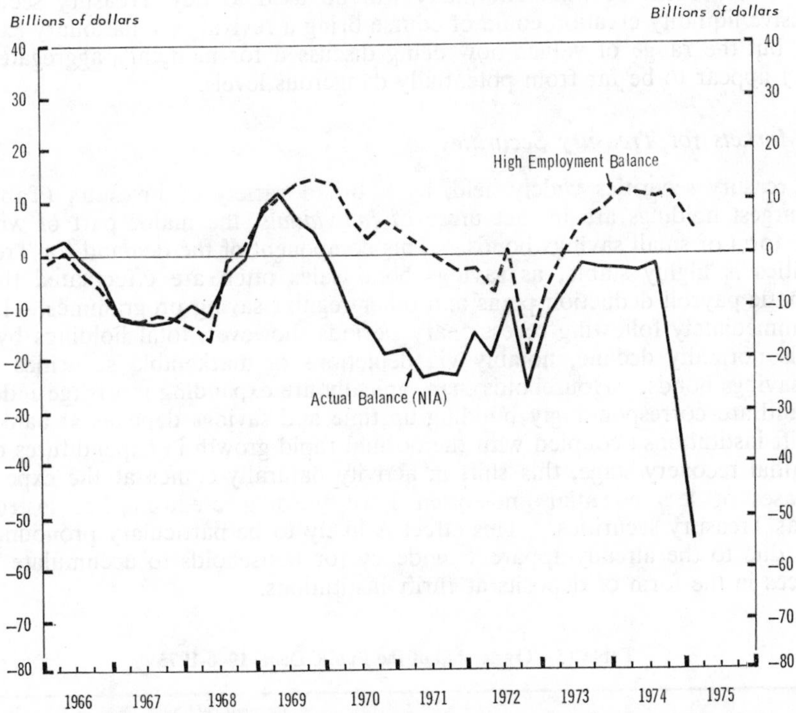

Billions of dollars   Billions of dollars

Source: Federal Reserve Bank of St. Louis; 1975-1976 figures are estimated. Data differ somewhat in methodology from those used in Table 7.

higher and higher interest rates to induce investors to buy securities. In so doing, the Treasury naturally must compete with other potential borrowers, including state and local governments, Federal agencies, and households in their capacity as purchasers of homes and consumer durables, as well as the corporate sector. The increased level of Treasury borrowing normally would drive up the rates which each of these other groups must pay, as it bids funds away that might have been used to purchase their new issues. The result is that interest-sensitive sectors could be discouraged from carrying out part of their planned borrowing activity so long as the cost of raising funds was high and rising. In short, these sectors could be partially crowded out of the capital markets by the unusually high Treasury borrowing.

This « crowding-out » effect could eventually reduce the expansionary effects of the fiscal actions, but it does not appear to be large enough to be serious in the near term. Because of the currently depressed level of private investment and a relatively strong propensity to save, the private sectors of the economy generally have sufficient financial ressources available, as described in the following paragraphs. And to the extent that interest rates might be pushed upward, there remains the possibility for accomodating monetary policies. The Federal Reserve can act directly to increase the total demand for Treasury securities simply by buying a larger quantity of such issues from securities dealers (open market operations). This activity, perhaps supplemented by reductions in cash reserve requirements for commercial banks or other instrumental changes[20], also provides commercial banks and, indirectly, the non-bank sectors of the economy with additional funds, some of which normally will be used to buy Treasury securities. Excessive liquidity creation could of course bring a revival of inflationary expectations, but the range of values now being discussed for monetary aggregates (see below) appear to be far from potentially dangerous levels.

The Markets for Treasury Securities

Treasury securities widely held, by a broad variety of investors (Table 15). The largest holdings are in fact those of *individuals,* the major part of which is in the form of small savings bonds. This component of the demand for Treasury securities is highly stable, as savings bond sales often are effectuated through automatic payroll deduction plans and other regular saving programmes. During and immediately following recessionary periods, however, total holdings by individuals normally decline, notably via depletions of marketable securities rather than savings bonds. Households then typically are expanding mortgage indebtedness and are correspondingly building up time and savings deposits at banks and at thrift institutions ; coupled with the normal rapid growth in expenditures during the initial recovery stage, this shift in activity naturally comes at the expense of purchases of less essential and often lower-yielding credit-market instruments such as Treasury securities. This effect is likely to be particulary pronounced in 1975, due to the already-apparent tendency for households to accumulate liquid balances in the form of deposits at thrift institutions.

Table 15   Ownership of the Public Debt, 1946-1975

End of year	Total amount ($ billion)	Per cent held by					
		Individuals	Corporations[2]	State and local govts.	Foreign investors	Commercial banks	Other investors[3]
1946[1]	231.6	27.6	23.9	2.9	1.0	40.5	4.1
1966	219.2	33.9	13.4	11.1	6.6	26.2	8.8
1972	262.5	28.2	7.5	11.0	21.0	25.8	6.5
1974	271.0	31.3	7.2	10.8	21.5	20.8	8.4
1975	345	23	12	8½	18	26½	12

1 End of February 1946 (immediate post-war peak in public debt).
2 Non-financial corporations plus insurance companies and mutual savings banks.
3 Savings and loan associations, non-profit institutions, corporate pension trust funds, dealers and brokers, and certain government accounts.
Source: Treasury Bulletin. 1975 figures are Secretariat estimates.

For most of the post-war period, the *non-financial business* sector has exhibited a tendency to decumulate government securities, though this downward trend has been reversed since 1970. Corporate holdings are largely short- and medium-term bills and notes, apparently held primarily for liquidity purposes. As alternative instruments, such as commercial paper and certificates of deposit, have emerged, the attractiveness of Treasury issues has declined. But there are a number of reasons to expect a sizeable accumulation by this sector in 1975 and perhaps into 1976. Although profits generally remain depressed, the total inflow of funds to corporations appears to be falling relatively

20   For a full description of the available instruments and their use, see OECD Monetary Studies Series, *Monetary Policy in the United States,* 1974.

less than is gross investment expenditure. The corporate sector thus is now in a relatively flush financial position. Alternative outlets for financial investment, furthermore, seem less attractive at the moment, due to the risks which have appeared in the past two years.

State and local governments add to their portfolios of Federal securities only slowly and sporadically, and usually only in periods of surplus in their own budgets. They are unlikely to be a significant factor in the forthcoming financing. The same conclusion holds, though for different reasons, for the *foreign* sector. This latter has displayed a dramatic growth since the mid-1960's, and now stands as one of the most important groups of investors in Treasury securities. For example, in 1971 — which saw the largest increase in Treasury debt of the post-war period, until the current year — net purchases by the foreign sector more than absorbed the total rise in publicly-held debt[21].

In general, funds for the purchase of Treasury securities by foreigners could come from a deficit in the current account of the balance of payments, an increase in gross capital outflows, portfolio shifts by foreigners in favour of Treasury issues, or some types of official transactions. The first source is unlikely to be significant for 1975, the projection now being for a current-account surplus, though a modest deficit may emerge in the second half. Shifts within the capital account may favour Treasury securities, if interest rates rise as expected later in the year or if oil exporters place part of the addition to their financial assets in this form. However, the extent of interest-sensitive capital inflows could be limited by investor or central-bank resistance should a significant appreciation of dollar exchange rates materialise. It also is important to note, given that the Federal Reserve could be expected to offset the effects of bank-related capital flows on the stock of money, that such portfolio shifts would inevitably draw funds away from other US liabilities. During the early months o this year, there have been some net purchases of (mostly non-marketable) securities by foreign accounts, most importantly by European central banks. But it is highly uncertain whether this movement may be expected to continue in the coming months.

The role of the *commercial banking system* in the Treasury securities market has been declining in importance gradually for the past thirty years ; bank holdings of Treasury issues have been virtually flat for the past 25 years. The low yields on government debt relative to returns on other assets (especially loans and tax-free municipal securities), the rapid growth in business demands for bank credit throughout this period, and an increasing emphasis on liquidity management by banks all have combined to reduce the portion of commercial bank assets held in the form of Treasury securities from 43 per cent at the end of 1950 to less than 7 per cent at the end of 1974.

This secular pattern is likely to be reversed sharply in 1975 and 1976. A number of large banks, concerned about the dangerously large losses incurred by a few banks in 1974, have initiated deliberate programmes to reduce the pace at which they extend loans to businesses and even to reduce their overall growth rate. In the first four months of 1975, commercial and industrial loans of large banks (seasonally adjusted) actually fell by some $10 billion, or at an annual rate of more than 20 per cent. Abetting this portfolio shifting, has been a drop in corporate demands for bank loans, as noted in the discussion above : the non-financial business sector is relying more heavily for the moment on longer-term debt financing, and especially on the bond market. So long as this trend continues, commercial bank demands for Treasury and other securities should account for a major portion of the growth in bank credit.

---

21 Public debt held by private investors (i.e. other than by Federal government accounts) rose by $ 18 billions in 1971, while foreign and international ownership rose by $ 23.6 billion.

Table 16   Sources of Growth in Bank Credit, 1967-1975

$ billion

	Demand deposits	Time deposits[1]	Negotiable CD's	Capital and credit markets[2]	Total Sources	Demand and time deposits as per cent of total
Average						
1967-1972	11.1	21.2	4.8	7.7	44.8	72.1
1973	13.0	30.3	20.0	25.3	88.6	48.9
1974	-2.6	26.6	28.6	12.4	65.0	36.9
1975	16½	43	-8	10	61½	97

1   Exclusive of negotiable CDs.
2   Equities, bonds, net interbank and miscellaneous liabilities, plus the excess of current surplus over gross physical investment.
Source: Federal Reserve System, Flow of Funds Accounts. 1975 figures are Secretariat estimates.

It is at this point that the monetary policies of the *Federal Reserves System* come into play.   Monetary expansion through open market operations directly absorbs part of the public debt into the central bank's portfolio, and expansion via any instrumental action enables the banking system to purchase additional securities and other assets.   In order to generate the magnitude of monetary growth envisaged for 1975 (Table 17), the Federal Reserve will have to expand the monetary base (currency plus bank reserves) by more than $6 billion, no doubt primarily through open market security purchases.   Barring significant shifts in other factors affecting bank reserves (such as Treasury deposits or currency, foreign deposits, Federal Reserve float), and assuming that there are no changes in reserve requirements other than those already announced, the Federal Reserve therefore may be expected to acquire at least $6 billion of Treasury issues for its own account in 1975[22].   As of mid-May, net purchases since the beginning of the year totalled some $3.5 billion.

Table 17   Growth in Monetary Aggregates, 1967-1975

Average	M1	M2	M3
1967-1972	6.5	8.8	9.2
1973	6.1	8.8	8.8
1974	4.7	7.4	6.8
1975	6½	10	11½

NOTE M_1 = stock of money (currency plus demand deposits).
M_2 = M_1 plus time deposits at commercial banks other than large CDs.
M_3 = M_2 plus deposits at non-bank thrift institutions.
Source: Federal Reserve Board, *Federal Reserve Bulletin*. 1975 figures are derived from the maximum values for official target growth rates.

22   Net purchases for the first five months of the year totalled some $ 4 billion, but the data for May are distorted by shifts in Treasury deposits due to the tax rebate.   The Treasury added about $ 6 billion to its deposit balances at Federal Reserve banks during April and early May in anticipation of the rebates, and then reduced these balances by more than $ 7 billion in the following month.   In order to prevent these transfers from temporarily drainings funds away from bank reserve balances, the Federal Reserve System made substantial open-market purchases and sales during this period.

As the Federal Reserve purchases securities, it directly creates reserves and deposits for commercial banks and provides them with the ability to further expand the stocks of money and bank credit. But as shown in Table 16, there is substantial scope for slippage here. During the late 1960's and early 1970's commercial banks were able to raise some $45 billion per year in new funds ; almost half came from ordinary time deposits and another fourth from demand deposits, with negotiable certificates of deposit (CDs) and miscellaneous sources being of relatively little importance. But in the past few years, total growth has been much higher, even though monetary growth as usually defined has been somewhat below average ; credit market instruments, including CDs and borrowings from foreign branches and other banks abroad, have accounted for much of the difference. Thus for 1973 and 1974, demand and ordinary time deposits combined covered well under half of total credit growth.

This situation is now being reversed. Monetary policy has been directed, since the third quarter of 1974, towards easier money-market conditions and increased growth in monetary aggregates. However, the response of the growth in money supply (M¹) was until recently rather sluggish, for a variety of reasons. First, the easing of money-market conditions has been achieved with relatively little expansion of bank reserves, due to a voluntary shift of deposit demand in favour of thrift institutions and the sharp reduction in corporate demands for bank credit in recent months. Second, the tapering of economic activity has lowered the demand for money balances for transactions purposes, so that time and savings deposits have grown fairly rapidly even while demand deposit balances have declined. Third, the drop in demand for bank credit has eliminated the impulse for banks to seek funds agressively through credit and capital markets. The stock of negotiable CDs grew only at slow rates in the second half of 1974 and has been declining since the turn of the year ; borrowings from Federal Reserve banks, which had attained exceptionally high levels by mid-1974 even excluding the loans to the troubled Franklin National Bank, have been near zero since late January ; Euro-dollar liabilities of domestic banks have been generally falling since December ; and other market sources of funds appear to have shown little change recently.

If the Federal Reserve System is able to generate monetary growth near the maximum values of its target ranges, the increase in the money stock (M₁) for 1975 will be roughly in line with or slightly above its trend value over the past decade, and commercial banks will thereby enjoy a healthy rise in demand deposit volume. Time and savings deposits should grow more rapidly in response to the combined sluggishness in aggregate demand and the continuation of expansionary monetary policies. But the outstanding volume of CDs can be expected to decline, while other credit market instruments may show only slight increases. Overall growth in bank credit is therefore likely to be below normal with almost all of the increase — in contrast to recent years — being " financed " by, or reflected in the more traditional deposit sources.

The prospect, then, is that commercial banks will be able to acquire just over $60 billion of financial assets of all kinds in 1975, a figure that is low in relation to recent years (Table 18). But the more important feature of bank credit growth this year would appear to be the shift in the composition of assets being acquired by the banks. Even allowing for a revival of mortgage demands in the second half of the year and a continued expansion of consumer credit requirements, total loan volume will be depressed by the drop in demands from the corporate sector. If the trend towards debt consolidation by corporations which has been so evident in the first half should continue throughout the year, there may occur virtually no net new bank lending to that sector during the year. So without crowding out potential borrowers, the banking system should be able to effect a substantial

Table 18   Asset Formation by Commercial Banks, 1967-1975

	Increase in financial assets ($ bill.)	Per cent of total in the form of				
		Treasury securities	Other securities[1]	Loans	Other credit[2]	Reserves and other cash
Average						
1967-1972	48.6	3.8	23.9	56.7	9.6	6.0
1973	100.2	−8.8	13.8	82.3	2.9	9.8
1974	73.6	−3.7	11.8	74.5	17.0	0.4
1975	61½	57	13	30	−3	3

1   State and local government obligations, securities of federally sponsored agencies, and corporate bonds.
2   Open-market paper, security credit, corporate equities, and miscellaneous assets.
Sources: Federal Reserve System, Flow of Funds Accounts.   1975 figures are Secretariat estimates.

portfolio shift in favour of Treasury securities, absorbing perhaps as much as $35 billion of the expected $80 billion increase in the public debt.

The final group of investors to be considered is the *non-bank financial sector,* including thrift institutions, insurance companies, pension funds, and various security dealers and investment funds.   This sector now holds about $60 billion of Treasury securities, so it is comparable in importance to the commercial banks. And in contrast to the latter, it has been adding significantly to its holdings in recent years (Table 19).   It is reasonable to expect these institutions to continue to accumulate securities for at least the next several months, for two reasons. First, the bulk of the loans made by this sector are mortgages, and the demands for both residential and non-residential construction remain weak and are expected to show only a mild recovery in the second half of the year.   Total loan demand may be buoyed slightly by inflation but probably will rise no more rapidly than in 1974.   Second, the supply of funds is rising very strongly, especially at thrift institutions.   Deposit and share accounts rose at a seasonally adjusted annual rate of 16 per cent in the first four months of 1975, and the high growth rates projected for M₂ (Table 4) over the rest of the year imply a continuation of that trend.   There thus will be a very large gap between growth of available funds at thrift institutions and the demand for loans, a significant portion of which is likely to be filled by net purchases of Treasury securities .

An important implication of the major role to be played by the non-bank financial sector is that it may enable the Treasury to issue above-average portions

Table 19   Asset Formation by the Non-Bank Financial Sector, 1967-1975

	Increase in financial assets ($ bill.)	Per cent of total in the form of				
		Treasury securities	Other securities[1]	Loans	Other credit[2]	Reserves and other cash
Average						
1967-1972	75.8	2.5	18.2	41.8	36.3	1.2
1973	87.7	1.0	16.5	64.8	15.3	2.4
1974	77.2	7.5	32.8	47.2	9.8	2.7
1975	108	21	33	32	11	3

1   State and local government obligations, securities of federally sponsored agencies, and corporate bonds.
2   Open-market paper, security credit, corporate equities, and miscellaneous assets.
Source: Federal Reserve System, Flow of Funds Accounts.   1975 figures are Secretariat estimates.

of longer-term securities. Commercial banks, non-financial corporations and foreign investors exhibit a preference for short-term assets such as Treasury bills ; well over half of their total holdings of Treasury issues are scheduled to mature within one year. The non-bank financial sector, on the other hand, holds the vast bulk of its portfolios in medium- and long-term maturities. Some care will have to be taken to ensure that mortgage institutions are not distracted from freely meeting available loan demands, as could follow from excessive concentration by the Treasury on longer-term issues. Nonetheless, the government should be able to float a broad variety of new issues throughout the maturity range this year. Flexible public debt management policies would not only reduce the risk of a " crowding-out " of any particular private sector but would also facilitate the achievement of short- and medium-term monetary growth targets.

Some Concluding Remarks

In summary, it would appear that the economy should have available the resources to purchase the debt obligations being issued by the Treasury during 1975 and to satisfy the other credit demands associated with the expected growth in aggregate demand, provided that monetary policy is adequately expansive. The maximum values of the Federal Reserve's target ranges for monetary growth are perhaps a bit scanty in their implications for total growth in bank credit associated with the forecast expansion of nominal GNP. In the event that demands for credit should become more buoyant than now foreseen, these target ranges could be revised upward somewhat without inducing an explosion of credit or a revival of inflationary pressures.

This generally sanguine outlook must be tempered with a little caution. The most immediate concern is that the existing portfolio composition for all financial sectors of the economy is being pushed very noticeably out of shape. It is not difficult to imagine some resistance by commercial banks, for example, to the placement of more than half of the increase in their available funds into a single type of asset (Treasury securities), particularly at the present relatively low yields. A rise in Treasury yields relative to state and local obligations and private claims may therefore be required. The second concern arises as on looks ahead to 1976. Assuming the continuation of current fiscal policies and some recovery in aggregate demand, the financial positions of the private sector will become tighter and private credit demands will begin to grow more rapidly. The corresponding rise in tax revenues and declines in unemployment benefits should then reduce the level of government budget deficits. If, however, the borrowing requirements of the public sector were to remain near present levels much beyond the middle of 1976 — which on present trends and policies seems unlikely — the entire structure of interest rates would probably begin a steep new ascent, discouraging corporate and household borrowers. The initiation of the coming recovery requires a large deficit, but its sustainment eventually will require an expansion of private investment and therefore some restoration of more normal financial patterns.

IV CONCLUSIONS

Inflation, one of the most important problems that has ailed the US economy in recent years, has now been brought down to a more manageable level, but the costs in terms of lost output and employment have been considerable. Production has been falling for more than a year and is now down to a level already attained three years ago and the unemployment rate is the highest since the pre-war depression. As the current advance of prices is still fast by past US standards, the authorities are aiming at a recovery which, though relatively moderate in view of existing unused capacity, should take up some slack by the middle of next year. Progress towards better price stability and higher employment levels may, however, be difficult to achieve without a responsive policy performance.

The experience of the last few years provides important lessons for the future. Excessive domestic demand pressures during the last boom were a major factor sparking off the acceleration of inflation in 1973, illustrating again the fact that maintenance of a reasonable degree of price stability requires improved demand management. And the perhaps unintentionally tight policy stance maintained during most of 1974 has been a major reason for the present cumulative downturn of the economy. While a perfectly steady growth of aggregate demand at the desired level of resource utilization is hardly attainable, there would nevertheless seem to be considerable scope for improvement in relation to the performance of the last decade.

Given the uncertainties and fluctuations to which modern economies are subject, prompt policy response may be essential to an acceptable degree of stability. The sharp upturn in demand in the second half of 1972 and the marked weakening in the fourth quarter of 1974 show that demand conditions may shift very rapidly. In some cases statistical indicators may not have provided reliable information as to the most current developments, and improvement may be possible in this area. However, even with the most reliable economic indicators, rapid policy action may be needed to avoid undesirable swings in demand. As in most countries, changes in monetary policy can be effected quickly, but these usually influence demand with an important time lag. However, as noted in previous OECD Surveys of the United States, shifts in fiscal policy may take considerable time and thus tend to come too late from the point of view of good demand management. More flexible arrangements have been introduced in many other Member countries and have helped importantly to reduce undesirable fluctuations in demand. Given the weight of the United States in the world economy, it may be particularly appropriate that flexible instruments of demand management be available.

The possible need for quick policy adjustment is well illustrated by the uncertainties pertaining to the short-term outlook. Given the stimulative measures that have been taken, an upswing is likely to develop during the second half of the year. But the strength of the recovery is uncertain as the reactions of both consumers and investors to the policy measures are unusually difficult to predict in the present situation of exceptionally high rates of unemployment and unused capacity. The extensive postponement of purchases of durable goods and houses over the past $1\frac{1}{2}$ years could give rise to a sharp rebound at some stage, once consumer confidence improves, and the simultaneous start of large energy and other resource-base related investment projects could generate a new investment boom. From the point of view of maintaining an acceptable degree of price stability, quick action would then be needed to prevent an excessive increase in demand pressure. On the other hand, given the once-and-for-all nature of the recent tax cuts and the relatively cautious money supply targets that have been adopted the main immediate risk may be that the recovery will lose momentum in the course of 1976, warranting further measures to stimulate demand.

The importance of re-establishing a recovery sufficient to reduce the present degree of slack needs no stressing ; indeed, from the point of view of reducing unemployment, a more vigorous recovery might have been desirable, as the upturn envisaged at present may not reduce unemployment much over the next twelve months. A recovery of activity in the US is also essential from the international point of view, providing a welcome boost to world trade which would help to ease the balance of payments and domestic positions of many Member and non-member countries alike. But it is also important both from the national and international points of view to avoid a resurgence of inflationary pressures in the United States. It may therefore be advisable to aim at a more moderate recovery than typical of previous business cycles. Prompt policy response may be needed to bring the economy smoothly back to a sustainable path of full employment growth in non-inflationary conditions.

In view of the risk of a flattening out of the upturn in 1976, it may be imprudent to allow a rise in interest rates at an early stage of the recovery ; some adjustment of the monetary targets announced by the Federal Reserve may therefore prove necessary. Should additional stimulative measures be needed, it would probably be inappropriate to proceed much further with tax reductions, as their demand impact is difficult to predict in conditions of very high unemployment. Selective increases of employment-creating public expenditure (Federal and State) may be preferable. It must be hoped that considerations relating to the size of the budget deficit will not prevent a demand management policy necessary to achieve an adequate recovery of activity and improvement of labour market conditions. The budget deficit is to a large extent a reflection of the low level of activity, and would to that extent decline as the economy recovers. In any case, the size of the deficit or the way it is financed cannot be primary goals of economic policy. The main consideration at present must be to ensure a satisfactory general economic development; any financial developments, such as a build-up of liquidities in the economy which could be excessive in the medium-term, could be corrected once a sustainable recovery of activity has been firmly restored.

A particular feature of US policy-making concerns energy conservation. The United States accounts for over 50 per cent of the total energy consumption in the OECD area. It is therefore to be hoped that energy-saving measures will not be unduly delayed.

Following the major turnaround in 1973 the underlying US foreign balance of payments position has continued to improve. Apart from cyclical factors which have tended to restrain imports rather more than exports, the competitive position of the United States has clearly strengthened as a result of cumulative effects of dollar devaluations and a comparatively lower rate of inflation. Despite the apparent strength of the current account the dollar has weakened since mid-1974 against the currencies of a number of European countries, mainly because of interest rate differentials. During the forecast period the current account will probably deteriorate, as the United States can be expected to lead an upswing in world trade. At the same time, however, a probable relatively lower rate of inflation in the US and a likely narrowing of interest rate differentials may reverse the downward pressure on the dollar.

STATISTICAL ANNEX

Table A National Product and Expenditure in Current Prices

Billions of dollars; quarterly data seasonally adjusted at annual rates

	Personal consumption expenditures	Gross private domestic investment	New construction	Producers' durable equipment	Change in business inventories	Net exports of goods and services	Govt. purchases of goods and services	Federal	State and local	Gross national product
1958	290.1	60.9	37.4	25.0	-1.5	2.2	94.2	53.6	40.6	447.3
1959	311.2	75.3	42.1	28.4	4.8	.1	97.0	53.7	43.3	483.7
1960	325.2	74.8	41.0	30.3	3.6	4.0	99.6	53.5	46.1	503.7
1961	335.1	71.7	41.0	28.6	2.0	5.6	107.6	57.4	50.2	520.1
1962	355.1	83.0	44.6	32.5	6.0	5.1	117.1	63.4	53.7	560.3
1963	375.0	87.1	46.5	34.8	5.9	5.9	122.5	64.2	58.2	590.5
1964	401.2	94.0	48.3	39.9	5.8	8.5	128.7	65.2	63.5	632.4
1965	432.8	108.1	52.8	45.8	9.6	6.9	137.0	66.9	70.1	684.9
1966	466.3	121.4	53.5	53.1	14.8	5.3	156.8	77.8	79.0	749.9
1967	492.1	116.6	53.1	55.3	8.2	5.2	180.1	90.7	89.4	793.9
1968	536.2	126.0	60.4	58.5	7.1	2.5	199.6	98.8	100.8	864.2
1969	579.5	139.0	66.9	64.3	7.8	1.9	210.0	98.8	111.2	930.3
1970	617.6	136.3	67.3	64.4	4.5	3.6	219.5	96.2	123.3	977.1
1971	667.1	153.7	80.8	66.6	6.3	-.2	234.2	97.6	136.6	1 054.9
1972	729.0	179.3	95.1	75.7	8.5	-6.0	255.7	104.9	150.8	1 158.0
1973	805.2	209.4	104.2	89.8	15.4	3.9	276.4	106.6	169.8	1 294.9
1974	876.7	209.4	98.0	97.1	14.2	2.1	309.2	116.9	192.3	1 397.4
1971: 1st quarter	650.5	146.6	74.3	64.4	7.9	2.9	227.9	95.9	132.0	1 027.8
2nd quarter	662.1	154.0	79.4	66.5	8.1	-.2	231.3	96.2	135.1	1 047.3
3rd quarter	672.1	153.5	83.4	66.3	3.8	.1	235.7	97.9	137.8	1 061.3
4th quarter	683.8	160.8	86.0	69.4	5.4	-3.4	242.1	100.5	141.6	1 083.2
1972: 1st quarter	701.5	169.4	92.5	72.0	5.0	-7.1	251.1	105.6	145.5	1 115.0
2nd quarter	720.6	175.5	93.9	73.7	8.0	-6.9	253.8	105.9	147.9	1 143.0
3rd quarter	736.8	182.1	95.1	76.8	10.2	-4.8	255.1	102.7	152.4	1 169.3
4th quarter	757.2	190.2	98.9	80.3	11.0	-5.3	262.6	105.2	157.4	1 204.7
1973: 1st quarter	781.7	199.0	103.1	85.9	10.0	-.8	269.0	106.4	162.6	1 248.9
2nd quarter	799.0	205.1	104.9	89.4	10.7	.5	273.3	106.2	167.1	1 277.9
3rd quarter	816.3	209.0	106.0	91.1	11.8	6.7	276.9	105.3	171.6	1 308.9
4th quarter	823.9	224.5	102.9	92.6	28.9	9.3	286.4	108.4	177.9	1 344.0
1974: 1st quarter	840.6	210.5	99.7	93.9	16.9	11.3	296.3	111.5	184.8	1 358.8
2nd quarter	869.1	211.8	101.0	97.2	13.5	-1.5	304.4	114.3	190.1	1 383.8
3rd quarter	901.3	205.8	97.2	99.9	8.7	-3.1	312.3	117.2	195.1	1 416.3
4th quarter	895.8	209.4	94.1	97.5	17.8	1.9	323.8	124.5	199.3	1 430.9
1975: 1st quarter	916.3	164.6	88.0	94.6	-18.0	5.4	332.8	127.7	205.1	1 419.2

Source: US Department of Commerce, *Survey of Current Business.*

Table B National Product and Expenditure in Constant Prices
Billions of 1958 dollars; quarterly data seasonally adjusted at annual rates

	Personal consumption expenditures	Gross private domestic investment	New construction	Producers' durable equipment	Change in business inventories	Net exports of goods and services	Govt. purchases of goods and services	Federal	State and local	Gross national product
1958	290.1	60.9	37.4	25.0	-1.5	2.2	94.2	53.6	40.6	447.3
1959	307.3	73.6	40.9	27.9	4.8	.3	94.7	52.5	42.2	475.9
1960	316.1	72.4	39.3	29.6	3.5	4.3	94.9	51.4	43.5	487.7
1961	322.5	69.0	39.0	28.1	2.0	5.1	100.5	54.6	45.9	497.2
1962	338.4	79.4	41.7	31.7	6.0	4.5	107.5	60.0	47.5	529.8
1963	353.3	82.5	42.7	34.0	5.8	5.6	109.6	59.5	50.1	551.0
1964	373.7	87.8	43.3	38.7	5.8	8.3	111.2	58.1	53.2	581.1
1965	397.7	99.2	46.1	44.0	9.0	6.2	114.7	57.9	56.8	617.8
1966	418.1	109.3	45.3	50.1	13.9	4.2	126.5	65.4	61.1	658.1
1967	430.1	101.2	43.0	50.6	7.7	3.6	140.2	74.7	65.5	675.2
1968	452.7	105.2	46.6	52.2	6.4	1.0	147.7	78.1	69.6	706.6
1969	469.1	110.5	48.0	55.8	6.7	.2	145.9	73.5	72.4	725.6
1970	477.5	103.4	45.9	53.5	3.9	2.3	139.3	64.3	75.0	722.5
1971	496.4	111.1	52.3	53.5	5.3	-.5	139.3	60.9	78.4	746.3
1972	527.3	125.0	58.1	59.8	7.0	-3.0	143.1	61.0	82.1	792.5
1973	552.1	138.1	58.3	69.0	10.8	4.6	144.4	57.3	87.0	839.2
1974	539.5	126.7	50.2	67.8	8.7	9.0	146.0	56.5	89.5	821.2
1971: 1st quarter	490.1	107.9	49.2	52.2	6.5	1.5	137.5	60.2	77.3	736.9
2nd quarter	493.8	111.8	51.6	53.3	6.8	-.9	137.5	59.7	77.8	742.1
3rd quarter	497.7	109.9	53.5	53.0	3.4	-.1	139.7	61.3	78.4	747.2
4th quarter	504.1	114.8	54.6	55.6	4.6	-2.4	142.6	62.4	80.2	759.1
1972: 1st quarter	512.8	119.4	57.7	57.4	4.2	-4.9	143.8	62.9	80.9	770.9
2nd quarter	523.2	123.2	58.2	58.4	6.6	-3.6	143.8	62.5	81.3	786.6
3rd quarter	531.2	126.6	57.8	60.3	8.5	-1.4	141.8	59.5	82.4	798.1
4th quarter	542.2	130.9	58.7	63.3	8.8	-1.9	143.0	59.2	83.8	814.2
1973: 1st quarter	552.9	134.4	59.7	67.4	7.3	1.4	144.1	58.9	85.2	832.8
2nd quarter	553.7	136.3	59.2	69.2	7.8	3.5	143.9	57.7	86.2	837.4
3rd quarter	555.4	135.8	58.2	69.5	8.0	5.8	143.7	56.2	87.5	840.8
4th quarter	546.3	145.8	55.8	70.0	20.0	7.9	145.7	56.4	89.3	845.7
1974: 1st quarter	539.7	133.3	53.1	69.7	10.6	11.5	146.0	56.3	89.7	830.5
2nd quarter	542.7	130.3	52.3	69.9	8.2	8.2	145.8	56.3	89.5	827.1
3rd quarter	547.2	122.7	49.0	68.7	5.0	7.3	145.9	56.5	89.4	823.1
4th quarter	528.2	120.5	46.5	63.1	10.9	9.1	146.3	57.0	89.3	804.0
1975: 1st quarter	532.3	90.6	42.8	58.8	-11.0	11.0	148.3	58.0	90.3	782.3

Source: US Department of Commerce, Survey of Current Business.

Table C Monetary Indicators
Seasonally adjusted (in billions of dollars)

	Money Supply[1]			Gross Loans and Investments at Commercial Banks[3]			
	Total	Currency	Demand deposits	Total[3]	Loans[3] [4]	US Treasury	Securities Other[4]
1967 : December	186.9	40.4	146.5	352.0	231.3	59.4	61.3
1968 : December	201.5	43.4	158.1	390.2	258.2	60.7	71.3
1969⁵ : December	208.6	46.1	162.5	401.7	279.1	51.5	71.1
1970 : December	221.2	49.1	172.2	435.5	291.7	57.9	85.9
1971 : December	235.3	52.6	182.7	484.8	320.3	60.1	104.4
1972 : December	255.8	56.9	198.9	556.4	377.8	61.9	116.7
1973 : December	271.5	61.6	209.9	630.3	447.3	52.8	130.2
1974 : January	270.9	62.0	208.9	638.9	452.9	54.5	131.5
February	273.1	62.7	210.4	647.4	458.3	56.4	132.7
March	275.2	63.3	211.9	657.5	468.2	56.4	132.9
April	276.6	63.9	212.8	666.9	476.3	57.1	133.5
May	277.6	64.3	213.3	673.4	481.4	57.2	134.8
June⁶	280.0	64.6	215.4	677.5	484.5	56.4	136.6
July	280.5	64.8	215.7	687.5	494.8	55.9	136.8
August	280.7	65.5	215.3	693.9	501.5	55.3	137.1
September	281.1	65.9	215.3	689.9	500.2	52.3	137.4
October	282.2	66.5	215.7	690.8	502.0	49.8	139.0
November⁷	283.8	67.3	216.5	692.5	503.8	49.1	139.6
December	284.3	67.8	216.6	687.0	498.2	48.7	140.1
1975 : January	282.2	68.1	214.1	689.3	500.7	48.8	139.8
February	283.8	68.6	215.1	691.0	497.6	53.3	140.1
March	286.8	69.4	217.5	694.7	496.4	58.7	139.6
April				696.1	492.4	64.4	139.3

1 Average of daily figures.
2 Data are for last Wednesday of month.
3 Adjusted to exclude domestic commercial interbank loans.
4 Beginning June 30, 1971, Farmers Home Administration insured notes totalling approximately $ 700 million are included in " Other securities " rather than in " Loans ".
5 Beginning June, 1969, data for loans and investments at commercial banks revised to include all bank premises subsidiaries and other significant majority owned subsidiaries; earlier data include commercial banks only. Series also changed to include gross loans and investments without the deduction of valuation reserves rather than net of valuation reserves as done previously.
6 Data beginning June 30, 1974, include one large mutual savings bank that merged with a nonmember commercial bank. As of that date there were increases of about $ 500 million in loans, $ 100 million in " Other securities ", and $ 600 million iu " Total loans and investments ".
7 As of Oct. 31, 1974, " Total loans and investments " of all commercial banks were reduced by $ 1.5 billion in connection with the liquidation of one large bank. Reductions in other items were: " Total loans ", $ 1.0 billion (of which $ 0.6 billion was in " Commercial and industrial loans "), and " Other securities ", $ 0.5 billion. In late November " Commercial and industrial loans " were increased by $ 0.1 billion as a result of loan reclassifications at another large bank.

Source: Board of Governors of the Federal Reserve System, *Federal Reserve Bulletin.*

Table D **Federal Budget Trends, Fiscal Years 1968-1974**

Billions of dollars

	1968	1969	1970	Actual 1971	1972	1973	1974
RECEIPTS, NATIONAL INCOME BASIS							
Personal taxes and non-taxes	71.4	90.0	93.6	87.5	100.7	106.8	123.1
Corporate profits tax accruals	33.7	37.4	33.3	32.3	34.1	41.2	45.6
Indirect business tax and non-tax accruals	17.1	18.6	19.2	20.1	20.0	20.7	21.6
Contributions for social insurance	38.3	44.4	49.1	52.6	58.5	71.7	83.3
Total receipts, national income basis	160.6	190.4	195.2	192.5	213.2	240.4	273.6
EXPENDITURES, NATIONAL INCOME BASIS							
Purchases of goods and services	94.9	99.4	98.0	95.8	103.2	105.3	110.3
Defense	(75.9)	(78.0)	(77.0)	(73.1)	(73.6)	(74.2)	(75.4)
Non-defense	(18.9)	(21.4)	(21.0)	(22.7)	(29.5)	(31.0)	(34.9)
Transfer payments	44.8	50.7	56.8	69.7	78.6	89.4	104.2
Domestic (" to persons ")	(42.7)	(48.5)	(54.8)	(67.4)	(75.7)	(86.7)	(101.3)
Foreign	(2.1)	(2.2)	(2.0)	(2.3)	(2.8)	(2.7)	(2.9)
Grants-in-aid to State and local governments	17.8	19.2	22.6	26.8	32.6	40.2	41.5
Net interest paid	10.9	12.3	14.0	14.3	13.4	14.5	17.4
Subsidies less current surplus of Government enterprises	4.1	4.1	4.7	5.7	5.3	6.7	4.7
Wage accruals less disbursements	—	—	-.1	.1	—	-.5	.2
Total expenditures, national income basis	172.5	185.7	195.9	212.4	232.9	255.4	278.3
Excess of receipts (+) or expenditures (—), national income basis	-11.9	+4.7	-.7	-19.8	-19.7	-15.0	-4.7
High employment budget surplus or deficit	-13.0	+5.1	+11.7	+4.0	-3.6	-6.6	9.2

Source: Budget data for 1968-1974 are based on the estimates prepared by the Department of Commerce. High employment budget balances are estimated by the Federal Reserve Bank of St. Louis, and differ slightly from those estimated by the Council of Economic Advisers.

Table E   Balance of Payments, OECD Basis

Millions of dollars

	1965	1966	1967	1968	1969	1970	1971	1972	1973	1974
Exports, fob	26 461	29 310	30 666	33 626	36 414	41 947	42 754	48 768	70 277	97 081
Imports, fob	21 510	25 493	26 866	32 991	35 807	39 788	45 476	55 754	69 806	102 962
Trade balance	4 951	3 817	3 800	635	607	2 159	-2 722	-6 986	471	-5 881
Services, net[1][2]	2 259	1 051	861	1 411	738	772	2 554	975	3 853	9 054
Balance on goods and services	7 210	4 868	4 661	2 046	1 345	2 931	-168	-6 011	4 324	3 172
Private transfers, net	-676	-648	-868	-827	-923	-1 060	-1 063	-1 052	-1 250	-1 083
Official transfers, net[2]	-2 177	-2 277	-2 246	-2 115	-2 055	-2 196	-2 585	-2 745	-2 626	-3 377
Current balance	4 357	1 943	1 547	-896	-1 633	-325	-3 816	-9 808	448	-1 286
Long-term capital (excl. spec. trans.)	-5 750	-4 381	-4 821	-1 171	-1 915	-3 697	-6 970	-1 565	-1 765	-9 294
(a) Private[3]	-4 073	-2 718	-2 600	1 072	-405	-1 752	-4 420	-243	10	-7 728
(b) Official[2][4]	-1 677	-1 663	-2 221	-2 243	-1 510	-1 945	-2 550	-1 322	-1 775	-1 566
Basic balance	-1 393	-2 438	-3 274	-2 067	-3 548	-4 022	-10 786	-11 373	-1 317	-10 580
Non-monetary short-term private capital	578	-34	1	-223	389	892	-1 076	-589	-1 177	-751
Non-monetary short-term official capital	—	—	—	—	—	—	—	—	—	—
Errors and omissions	-494	64	-439	94	-1 805	-458	-9 776	-1 790	-2 303	5 197
Balance on non-monetary transactions	-1 309	-2 408	-3 712	-2 196	-4 964	-3 588	-21 638	-13 752	-4 797	-6 134
Private monetary institutions short-term capital	456	2 300	742	3 705	7 791	-7 362	-9 059	2 550	-797	-1 936
(a) Assets	325	-84	-730	-105	-867	-1 122	-2 368	-2 199	-5 043	-17 668
(b) Liabilities[5]	131	2 384	1 472	3 810	8 658	-6 240	-6 691	4 749	4 246	15 732
Balance on official settlements	-853	-108	-2 970	1 509	2 827	-10 950	-30 697	-11 202	-5 594	-8 070
Total liabilities to foreign national official agencies[6]	33	-964	3 344	-758	-1 541	7 815	27 427	10 866	5 095	9 504
Use of IMF credit[7]	34	177	22	-3	-11	-453	-22	-544	—	—
Special transactions[8]	-437	328	-447	132	-87	244	227	137	289	—
Miscellaneous official accounts	—	—	—	—	—	—	—	—	—	—
Allocation of SDRs	—	—	—	—	—	867	717	710	—	—
Change in reserves (+ = increase)	-1 222	-568	-52	880	1 187	-2 477	-2 348	-32	-209	1 434
(a) Gold	-1 665	-571	-1 170	-1 173	967	-787	-866	-547	—	-3
(b) Currency assets	349	540	1 024	1 183	-814	-2 152	-381	-35	-233	1 265
(c) Reserve positions in IMF	94	-537	94	870	1 034	-389	-1 350	-153	33	172
(d) Special Drawing Rights	—	—	—	—	—	851	249	703	-9	—

1 Includes debt obligations payable by the United Kingdom but waived ($ 70 million in 1965, $ 66 million in 1968), but excludes reinvested earnings.
2 Excluding transactions related to cancellation of Indian debt in 1974 Q1: investment income : 17 million, official transfers : — 2010 million, long-term off. capital: 1992 million in 1974 Q2 : excluding other extraordinary grants estimated at: off. transfers: —746 million official long-term capital: 746 million.
3 Includes changes in foreign long-term claims on US commercial banks. Excludes liquification of UK govt. portfolio ($ 520 million in 1965, $ 101 million in 1966 and $ 463 million in 1969).
4 Includes changes in investment by international organisations in US government agency bonds, includes debt obligations payable by the UK but waived ($ 68 million in 1965, $ 72 million in 1968).
5 Excludes liabilities to foreign national official agencies. Includes liquid liabilities of other sectors than banking sector to foreign non-official institutions and persons (including liquid liabilities to non-monetary international and regional organisations).
6 Includes liabilities to BIS.
7 Includes gold deposits and investment by the IMF.
8 *Special transactions*: 1965: Debt prepayments: $ 221 million, UK waiver: $ -138 million, liquification of UK Government portfolio: $ -520 million; 1966: Debt prepayments: $ 429 million, liquification of UK Government portfolio: $ 6 million, liquification of UK Government portfolio: $ -453 million; 1967: Debt prepayments: $ -101 million; 1968: Debt prepayments: $ 269 million; UK waiver: $ -137 million; 1969: Debt prepayments: $ 244 million; 1970: Debt prepayments: $ 226 million; 1971: Debt prepayments: $ 137 million; 1973: Debt prepayments: $ 289 million.

NOTE: Very recent revisions to balance of payments statistics, included in the shorter text table (10), have not been carried through in this table.

Sources: US Department of Commerce, *Survey of Current Business*; Federal Reserve System, *Federal Reserve Bulletin*.

INTERNATIONAL COMPARISONS

BASIC STATISTICS :

INTERNATIONAL COMPARISONS

OECD SALES AGENTS
DEPOSITAIRES DES PUBLICATIONS DE L'OCDE

ARGENTINA – ARGENTINE
Carlos Hirsch S.R.L.,
Florida 165, BUENOS-AIRES.
☎ 33-1787-2391 Y 30-7122

AUSTRALIA – AUSTRALIE
International B.C.N. Library Suppliers Pty Ltd.,
161 Sturt St., South MELBOURNE, Vic. 3205.
☎ 69.7601
658 Pittwater Road, BROOKVALE NSW 2100.
☎ 938 2267

AUSTRIA – AUTRICHE
Gerold and Co., Graben 31, WIEN 1.
☎ 52.22.35

BELGIUM – BELGIQUE
Librairie des Sciences
Coudenberg 76-78, B 1000 BRUXELLES 1.
☎ 512-05-60

BRAZIL – BRESIL
Mestre Jou S.A., Rua Guaipá 518,
Caixa Postal 24090, 05089 SAO PAULO 10.
☎ 256-2746/262-1609
Rua Senador Dantas 19 s/205-6, RIO DE
JANEIRO GB. ☎ 232-07. 32

CANADA
Information Canada
171 Slater, OTTAWA. KIA 0S9.
☎ (613) 992-9738

DENMARK – DANEMARK
Munksgaards Boghandel
Nørregade 6, 1165 KØBENHAVN K.
☎ (01) 12 69 70

FINLAND – FINLANDE
Akateeminen Kirjakauppa
Keskuskatu 1, 00100 HELSINKI 10. ☎ 625.901

FRANCE
Bureau des Publications de l'OCDE
2 rue André-Pascal, 75775 PARIS CEDEX 16.
☎ 524.81.67
Principaux correspondants :
13602 AIX-EN-PROVENCE : Librairie de
l'Université. ☎ 26.18.08
38000 GRENOBLE : B. Arthaud. ☎ 87.25.11
31000 TOULOUSE : Privat. ☎ 21.09.26

GERMANY – ALLEMAGNE
Verlag Weltarchiv G.m.b.H.
D 2000 HAMBURG 36, Neuer Jungfernstieg 21
☎ 040-35-62-500

GREECE – GRECE
Librairie Kauffmann, 28 rue du Stade,
ATHENES 132. ☎ 322.21.60

HONG-KONG
Government Information Services,
Sales of Publications Office,
1A Garden Road,
☎ H-252281-4

ICELAND – ISLANDE
Snaebjörn Jónsson and Co., h.f.,
Hafnarstræti 4 and 9, P.O.B. 1131,
REYKJAVIK. ☎ 13133/14281/11936

INDIA – INDE
Oxford Book and Stationery Co.:
NEW DELHI, Scindia House. ☎ 47388
CALCUTTA, 17 Park Street. ☎ 24083

IRELAND – IRLANDE
Eason and Son, 40 Lower O'Connell Street,
P.O.B. 42, DUBLIN 1. ☎ 01-41161

ISRAEL
Emanuel Brown :
35 Allenby Road, TEL AVIV. ☎ 51049/54082
also at :
9, Shlomzion Hamalka Street, JERUSALEM.
☎ 234807
48 Nahlath Benjamin Street, TEL AVIV.
☎ 53276

ITALY – ITALIE
Libreria Commissionaria Sansoni :
Via Lamarmora 45, 50121 FIRENZE. ☎ 579751
Via Bartolini 29, 20155 MILANO. ☎ 365083
Sous-dépositaires:
Editrice e Libreria Herder,
Piazza Montecitorio 120, 00186 ROMA.
☎ 674628
Libreria Hoepli, Via Hoepli 5, 20121 MILANO.
☎ 865446
Libreria Lattes, Via Garibaldi 3, 10122 TORINO.
☎ 519274
La diffusione delle edizioni OCDE è inoltre assicu-
rata dalle migliori librerie nelle città più importanti.

JAPAN – JAPON
OECD Publications Centre,
Akasaka Park Building,
2-3-4 Akasaka,
Minato-ku
TOKYO 107. ☎ 586-2016
Maruzen Company Ltd.,
6 Tori-Nichome Nihonbashi, TOKYO 103,
P.O.B. 5050, Tokyo International 100-31.
☎ 272-7211

LEBANON – LIBAN
Documenta Scientifica/Redico
Edison Building, Bliss Street,
P.O.Box 5641, BEIRUT. ☎ 354429 – 344425

THE NETHERLANDS – PAYS-BAS
W.P. Van Stockum
Buitenhof 36, DEN HAAG. ☎ 070-65.68.08

NEW ZEALAND – NOUVELLE-ZELANDE
The Publications Officer
Government Printing Office
Mulgrave Street (Private Bag)
WELLINGTON. ☎ 46.807
and Government Bookshops at
AUCKLAND (P.O.B. 5344). ☎ 32.919
CHRISTCHURCH (P.O.B. 1721). ☎ 50.331
HAMILTON (P.O.B. 857). ☎ 80.103
DUNEDIN (P.O.B. 1104). ☎ 78.294

NORWAY – NORVEGE
Johan Grundt Tanums Bokhandel,
Karl Johansgate 41/43, OSLO 1. ☎ 02-332980

PAKISTAN
Mirza Book Agency, 65 Shahrah Quaid-E-Azam,
LAHORE 3. ☎ 66839

PHILIPPINES
R.M. Garcia Publishing House,
903 Quezon Blvd. Ext., QUEZON CITY,
P.O. Box 1860 – MANILA. ☎ 99.98.47

PORTUGAL
Livraria Portugal,
Rua do Carmo 70-74. LISBOA 2. ☎ 360582/3

SPAIN – ESPAGNE
Libreria Mundi Prensa
Castelló 37, MADRID-1. ☎ 275.46.55
Libreria Bastinos
Pelayo, 52, BARCELONA 1. ☎ 222.06.00

SWEDEN – SUEDE
Fritzes Kungl. Hovbokhandel,
Fredsgatan 2, 11152 STOCKHOLM 16.
☎ 08/23 89 00

SWITZERLAND – SUISSE
Librairie Payot, 6 rue Grenus, 1211 GENEVE 11.
☎ 022-31.89.50

TAIWAN
Books and Scientific Supplies Services, Ltd.
P.O.B. 83, TAIPEI.

TURKEY – TURQUIE
Librairie Hachette,
469 Istiklal Caddesi,
Beyoglu, ISTANBUL, ☎ 44.94.70
et 14 E Ziya Gokalp Caddesi
ANKARA. ☎ 12.10.80

UNITED KINGDOM – ROYAUME-UNI
H.M. Stationery Office, P.O.B. 569, LONDON
SE1 9 NH, ☎ 01-928-6977, Ext. 410
or
49 High Holborn
LONDON WC1V 6HB (personal callers)
Branches at: EDINBURGH, BIRMINGHAM,
BRISTOL, MANCHESTER, CARDIFF,
BELFAST.

UNITED STATES OF AMERICA
OECD Publications Center, Suite 1207,
1750 Pennsylvania Ave, N.W.
WASHINGTON, D.C. 20006. ☎ (202)298-8755

VENEZUELA
Libreria del Este, Avda. F. Miranda 52,
Edificio Galipán, Aptdo. 60 337, CARACAS 106.
☎ 32 23 01/33 26 04/33 24 73

YUGOSLAVIA – YOUGOSLAVIE
Jugoslovenska Knjiga, Terazije 27, P.O.B. 36,
BEOGRAD. ☎ 621-992

6.75

Les commandes provenant de pays où l'OCDE n'a pas encore désigné de dépositaire
peuvent être adressées à :
OCDE, Bureau des Publications, 2 rue André-Pascal, 75775 Paris CEDEX 16
Orders and inquiries from countries where sales agents have not yet been appointed may be sent to
OECD, Publications Office, 2 rue André-Pascal, 75775 Paris CEDEX 16

DOCUMENTS OFFICIELS

■ ∴ 1979

GOVERNMENT
PUBLICATIONS

OECD   PUBLICATIONS
2, rue André-Pascal
75775 PARIS CEDEX 16
No. 35,047.   1975.

●

PRINTED   IN   FRANCE